D1522887

Dollar$ and Sense of Battlefield Preservation

The Economic Benefits of Protecting Civil War Battlefields

A Handbook for Community Leaders

Frances H. Kennedy and Douglas R. Porter
The Conservation Fund

The Preservation Press
National Trust for Historic Preservation
1785 Massachusetts Avenue, N.W., Washington, D.C. 20036

The National Trust for Historic Preservation is the only private, nonprofit organization chartered by Congress to encourage public participation in the preservation of sites, buildings, and objects significant in American history and culture. In carrying out this mission, the National Trust fosters an appreciation of the diverse character and meaning of our American cultural heritage and preserves and revitalizes the livability of our communities by leading the nation in saving America's historic environments.

Support for the National Trust is provided by membership dues, contributions, and a matching grant from the National Park Service, U.S. Department of the Interior, under provisions of the National Historic Preservation Act of 1966. The opinions expressed here do not necessarily reflect the views or policies of the Interior Department.

Copyright ©1994 The Conservation Fund.
All rights reserved. No part of this book may be reproduced in any manner without written permission from the publisher except for brief quotations used in reviews.

Printed in the United States of America
97 96 95 94   5 4 3 2 1

Library of Congress Cataloging in Publication Data
Dollarȿ and sense of battlefield preservation: the economic benefits of protecting Cival War battlefields: a handbook for community leader/the Conservation Fund, Frances H. Kennedy.
p. cm.
Includes bibliographical references (p.).
ISBN 0-89133-257-X
1. United States—History—Civil War, 1861-1865—Battlefields.
2. Battlefields—United States—Conservation and restoration—Economic aspects—Handbooks, manuals, etc. 3. Historic preservation—United States—Economic aspects—Handbooks, manuals, etc. I. Conservation Fund (Arlington, Va.) II. Kennedy, Frances H. III. Porter, Douglas R.
E641.D65 1994
973.7'6—dc20   94-25733
CIP

Design by Rock Creek Publishing Group
Front Cover Photo: Antietam National Battlefield, © 1994 Eric Long
Rear Cover Photo: The Clara Barton Monument,
Antietam National Battlefield, © 1994 Brad H. Keller

The *Dollar$ and Sense of Battlefield Protection* provides factual, well-documented information that makes a compelling case for protecting battlefields—and indeed, critical open space of all kinds.

Jean Hocker
President, Land Trust Alliance, Washington, D.C.

•••

The *Dollar$ and Sense of Battlefield Preservation* will be an invaluable tool for communities committed to the successful union of economic development and preservation of cultural and natural resources.

Sandra Ford Fulton
Commissioner, State Department of Tourist Development,
Nashville, Tennessee

•••

Congratulations on the production of this valuable handbook! Spotsylvania County, with four major Civil War battlefields, has gone through the struggle to balance battlefield preservation and economic development that is described in your handbook. Fortunately, more and more county residents and officials are embracing the prescription you outline. Other communities that are starting to see pressure on Civil War battlefields will be well served by this handbook. I only wish it had been available sooner.

L. Kimball Payne III
County Administrator, Spotsylvania County, Virginia

•••

Contrary to its title, this book is about much more than protecting Civil War battlefields. It is about a way of looking at community investment that preserves its natural resources, honors its precious heritage, and creates innovative cultural laboratories for people of all ages—all of this while being fiscally responsible in a way that makes more traditional projects with higher short term yields seem irresponsible by comparison. In addition to being a blueprint for historic preservation, it is also a guideline for the low impact economics of long-term sustainability.

Steven Bingler
Concordia Architects, New Orleans, Louisiana

•••

The Dollars and Sense of Battlefield Preservation persuasively refutes the misconception that there is an inherent conflict between the economic needs of a community and the preservation of battlefields. It will prove extremely useful to public officials and private citizens concerned with the preservation of some of our nation's most important memorial landscapes.

Reuben M. Rainey
School of Architecture, University of Virginia

•••

Contents

Acknowledgments

We thank first Herb McLaughlin, whose vision and support made this publication possible.

This handbook is the result of a broad public-private partnership. Special thanks go to the National Trust for Historic Preservation, The Hoblitzelle Foundation, The Gilder Foundation, and Mr. and Mrs. John L. Nau, III. We are grateful to the many people, now too many to name individually, who gave their time to read the manuscript, make suggestions, and provide information. We also appreciate the generous help from the Land Trust Alliance and from Katherine Boonin Andrus. Our final thanks go to Jack Lynn, Megan Susman, and Sally Case at The Conservation Fund, who kept the book moving forward, and to Patrick F. Noonan, the Fund's chairman, whose ideas launched this publication. We claim as our own any errors in the book.

Frances H. Kennedy
Douglas R. Porter
August 1994

Foreword

The battlegrounds of the Civil War define the character of many American communities. But the country
meadows where armies clashed, where bravery and sacri-
fice made farm fields nationally important historic monuments, are today at the edges of residential and industrial
growth. Community leaders are being asked to choose between apparently incompatible goals - preservation or economic development. Fortunately, as you will see in the
pages that follow, that threat of incompatibility is a myth.

Communities that plan development to complement
the historic treasures that battlefields represent benefit in
many ways. Publicly and privately protected battlefields
act like "basic industries." They generate jobs and income.
They produce tax surpluses for local government. At the
same time, they provide open space and help preserve the
quality of life for residents new and old.

Preserving historic land, creating greenways, and
protecting wildlife habitat can all provide positive economic benefits. As a nation we are beginning to understand the values and necessity of blending economic and
preservation goals. This realization is vital to meeting the
complex choices facing communities as we move toward
the 21st century. At The Conservation Fund, we believe
that by forming partnerships and integrating economic and
environmental policies, we demonstrate a new and better
approach for America that will sustain our communities
and build a better life for all our citizens.

Patrick F. Noonan
Chairman
The Conservation Fund

III

A Letter from the Front Line:

Maury County, Tennessee, has been and is going through a period of rapid development. Industrial and commercial developers, followed closely by residential developers, have found out what those of us who have lived here for years know—that Maury County has a lot to offer in natural resources, beauty, and heritage. So many times developers forget what draws them to an area and fail to protect those things that make development profitable. Local landowners too often sell out before the long-term consequences are considered.

The Dollar$ and Sense of Battlefield Preservation handbook is essential to any community involved in planning the open land available in their area whether battlefields are involved or not. I wish that everyone in our county involved in planning or owning land that may some day be developed could read this document. Education of landowners is a must to do proper planning in any community, and this handbook is an excellent tool for that purpose.

Maury County has battlefields that need preserving, and they are located in communities that also need preserving. It is my belief that this handbook will aid in accomplishing this goal. This is a well written and informative handbook, and I appreciate your sharing it with me.

A. C. Howell
Director of Accounts and Budgets, Maury County, Columbia, Tennessee

Preface

Ideas Worth Dollar$ to
Community Leaders

This handbook for community leaders
is about one aspect of Civil War battlefields: their effect on economic growth.

*— Does your community need an expanded tax
base to generate current revenue?*

*— Does your county need a more diversified
economy to ensure long-term prosperity?*

Your Civil War battlefield can help achieve these
goals—if you protect it. Preservation of your battlefield can
be a reliable, cost-effective alternative to the massive outlays
of tax dollars for roads, utilities, and public services demanded
by residential, commercial, and industrial development.

As a community leader you are compelled to walk a
tightrope, balancing short-term revenue with long-range
planning. The decisions you make today will affect your
community for generations to come. Your battlefield can
reward you—in dollars, jobs, and community heritage—if
you plan ahead so that development is away from, instead
of on, the battlefield.

> There are many benefits to be gained from planning
> to preserve your community's heritage:
> - greater diversification in your local economy
> - a more attractive place to live and work
> - the net profit in tax revenue that open space can generate
> - increased land values that a historic area can generate
> - an agreed upon vision of your community's future

In short, your battlefield can be a fiscal asset if it is protected. Moreover, your historic land can create an attractive basic industry for your community: heritage tourism.

The emphasis in *Dollar$ and Sense* is on taking an active role in making your battlefield a positive force in your community. Here is what you will learn:
- A battlefield can be a basic industry that generates jobs in your community.
- Battlefields can generate income: from visitors, from the park's expenditures, from sales tax on visitors' purchases.
- Historic open space can add value to adjacent properties.
- Protected open space enhances the community's environment.
- In contrast to open space, development can cost more than it generates in taxes, forcing you, the community's leaders, to raise property taxes.

Data collected from Civil War battlefields show the gains that can flow from battlefield preservation. The following are some of the highlights:

Battlefields can bring income into communities from visitor expenditures.
- Visitors to Pea Ridge National Military Park in Arkansas spent $10.8 million in 1991.
- Each visitor in 1992 to Wilson's Creek National Battlefield in Missouri spent an average of $49 per day.

Battlefields drew about 10 million visitors in 1993.
- Gettysburg, Pennsylvania: 1,199,200
- Harpers Ferry, West Virginia: 449,300
- Perryville, Kentucky: 265,970

> Battlefields bring income into communities through the *multiplier effect* of visitor expenditures: Every dollar a visitor spends is multiplied—spent again in the community—by an average of two times.
> - At Pea Ridge, Arkansas, $10.8 million in visitor expenditures have a total economic effect from visitor spending of $20.2 million.

> Battlefields bring money into communities through expenditures by the management of the battlefield:
> - The National Park Service spent nearly $1.6 million at Petersburg, Virginia, and $792,500 at Kennesaw Mountain, Georgia.
> - Expenditures for management of state-owned battlefields amounted to $179,716 at Port Hudson, Louisiana, and $154,683 at Bentonville, North Carolina.

Money brought into communities by battlefields creates jobs, just like other basic industries. Battlefields generate tax revenue for communities through sales taxes on visitors' purchases. Every dollar of business sales to visitors generates about 7.3 cents of state and local tax revenue.
- Historic Fredericksburg generated $893,000 in sales tax revenue last year.

Battlefields can increase the value of adjacent land. Everyone knows that the building lots next to a golf course are more valuable than those a block away. The same can be true for other protected open space, including battlefields.

Even privately owned battlefields—that can be viewed from public roads but are not open to the public— can be a fiscal asset to a community.

Here is what we know about the cost of public services per dollar of tax revenue:
- In Culpeper County, Virginia, open land costs the county 17 cents of every dollar it generates in taxes. In contrast, residential properties cost $1.25 for every dollar they pay in real estate taxes. So in Culpeper County,

open land generates a net surplus of 83 cents for every tax dollar paid, while residential properties result in a 25-cent deficit for every tax dollar paid.

- In Beekman, New York, the open space "profit" is 52 cents compared with the deficit of 12 cents on every dollar a residence pays in real estate taxes.

New development can mean higher taxes for long-time residents.

The hidden costs of new development can be substantial. Although commercial development is supposed to generate tax surpluses, it can result in a deficit if it also spawns residential development. Before assuming that commercial development will mean an automatic net tax surplus, communities need to look closely at the kind of development being proposed and whether it will require new housing. Broadening the tax base can mean higher taxes, not lower.

- In two Virginia counties, houses that are valued at less than $300,000 cost more in services for schools, roads, and utilities than they pay in real estate taxes.
- In Albemarle County, Virginia, although the population grew by 18 percent and the real estate tax base expanded by 44 percent, real estate taxes still increased by 78 percent.

The final sections of *Dollar$ and Sense* can help communities develop a better strategy by

- planning for battlefield preservation *and* development
- balancing community interests with private interests

•••

This impressive analysis will be useful to planning commissions, council members, and supervisors whether or not they have battlefields in their jurisdiction. It should be required reading for all those involved in planning decisions. I am sure that this economic study will help to save threatened battlefields and open land as well.

Elizabeth G. Helm
Former Mayor, Winchester, Virginia

Introduction

Plain Talk about the Economic Benefits of Battlefield Preservation

Community leaders today are concerned about sustainability. This handbook is presented in response to their inquiries about how protecting battlefields can sustain their economy and their heritage. They are also interested in how to protect their historic land; how to evaluate the effects of preservation on their community's heritage, character, and economy; and how to develop effective partnerships among landowners, developers, nonprofits, corporations, public agencies, foundations, businesses, schools, and colleges.

This handbook highlights the challenges, economic costs, and benefits of protecting battlefields. It emphasizes partnerships and cooperation. It presents community strategies for evaluating the costs and benefits of preservation and of development on and near the "hallowed ground." Communities are learning to encourage developers who understand that historic preservation can increase the economic value of development. This handbook draws on the experience of leaders who have gathered citizens together to work cooperatively toward a vision of their community's future, one that honors their forebears and respects their children's heritage.

Four years of ferocious fighting in the U.S. Civil War turned farms and forests into battlefields that witnessed both glory and tragedy. There were nearly 400 important conflicts stretching across 20 states from New Mexico to Georgia, from Florida to Pennsylvania. Seven generations later, the struggle to preserve the remnants of that hallowed ground is ongoing.

While some of the significant battlefields have been saved for posterity, most of those protected by public agencies are too small to tell of the events and the soldiers who fought and died there. For example, the National Park Service (NPS) battlefield at Tupelo, Mississippi, is only one acre, yet 23,000 fought there and 2,000 were casualties; the one-acre battlefield at Brices Cross Roads, Mississippi, saw the military genius of Nathan Bedford Forrest result in a resounding Confederate victory involving 12,000 soldiers, 25 percent of whom were casualties. Many battlefields have disappeared completely.[1] Critical ones such as Brandy Station, Virginia, could be lost to development.

Americans care about Civil War battlefields. In 1992 more than 9.7 million people visited NPS battlefields.[2] Parents want their children to learn about the events that changed forever America's ideas about individual freedom and national unity. Descendants of the 3 million men who served come to see where their ancestors fought. Historians, military analysts, and Civil War buffs trace the battles on the terrain. Many Americans come simply to reflect on the circumstances that turned their forebears bitterly against one another. They treasure the meadows and monuments, forests and fortifications, that honor the soldiers, teach our history, and lend character to our communities.

Although concerns of hearts and minds are important, the value of Civil War battlefields can extend beyond such intangibles. Battlefields can be economic generators that provide quantifiable benefits to a community and enhance its quality of life. People enjoy living in historic places that have been preserved, that have "character," such as Santa Fe and Williamsburg, Harpers Ferry and Antietam. The appeal of these communities is rooted in their history—protected through the vision of previous generations.

As an economic force in the community, a battlefield can outperform many alternative uses of the land. Protected battlefields such as Appomattox and Port Hudson draw visitors who spend money for food, lodging, books, gasoline, and other commodities and services. Sales taxes generate tax revenue for local governments. Businesses that serve visitors create jobs, hire employees, and pur-

chase services from other area firms. The public agencies
that own and manage battlefields also bring money into
the area through both operating and capital expenditures.

Battlefields preserved by private landowners as farmland or other open space contribute value in terms of agricultural production, scenic opportunities, and
environmental protection. Owners of privately preserved
battlefields can generate significant tax revenue when the
real estate taxes they pay result in a net surplus in real estate taxes. Moreover, unlike residential, commercial, and
industrial development, there are no infrastructure costs for
roads, schools, water, and sewers associated with battlefields. A protected battlefield can, therefore, be a low risk,
low impact investment. It also can be a low capital, high
yield investment, unlike other forms of community investment with hidden costs that result in a net loss for the local
government and thus higher taxes for landowners.

Communities that benefit from battlefields also have
a stewardship responsibility. Leaders, landowners, and
public agencies must work in partnership to manage the
tourism and control development nearby. Careful, comprehensive planning will enable future visitors to experience the timeless qualities of the battlefield, unchanged by
the visitors who preceded them.

•••

The preservation vision was boldly stated by a great
man of the American outdoors, President Theodore
Roosevelt:

> Here is your country. Do not let anyone take
> it or its glory away from you. Do not let selfish
> men or greedy interests skin your country of its
> beauty, its riches, or its romance. The World and
> the Future and your very children shall judge you
> according to [the way] you deal with this Sacred
> Trust.

[1] Frances H. Kennedy, ed., *The Civil War Battlefield Guide* (Boston, 1990). The guide, a publication of The Conservation Fund, includes narratives, maps, and photographs relating to 60 battles, as well as information on land protected on each battlefield.

[2] National Park Service, *Annual Statistical Abstracts*, prepared by the Socio-Economic Division. The following list shows the number of visitors to Civil War sites in the NPS in 1992:

Gettysburg, Pa.	1,299,200
Chickamauga, Ga., and Chattanooga, Tenn.	995,600
Kennesaw Mountain, Ga.	926,800
Vicksburg, Miss.	910,500
Manassas, Va.	867,600
Richmond, Va.	473,100
Fredericksburg and Spotsylvania, Va.	472,600
Arlington House, Va.	459,700
Harpers Ferry, W.Va.	449,300
Shiloh, Tenn.	408,000
Fort Pulaski, Ga.	364,000
Fort Sumter, S.C.	337,200
Appomattox Courthouse, Va.	311,900
Petersburg, Va.	299,200
Stones River, Tenn.	243,800
Antietam, Md.	243,700
Fort Donelson, Tenn.	218,900
Wilson's Creek, Mo.	174,600
Andersonville, Ga.	143,000
Pea Ridge, Ark.	113,700
Brices Cross Roads, Miss.	not reporting
TOTAL	9,712,400

(Above) In 1907 this statue was dedicated to honor Colonel George W. Gowen, who fell leading his men on the battlefield at Petersburg.

(Below) A recent photograph of the statue and the hallowed ground, now the Walnut Mall, Petersburg, Virginia.

Part One

The Economic Benefits of Battlefield Preservation

A Civil War battlefield—whether protected and open to visitors or preserved by a private owner as open space—can be a significant component of a community's economy, yielding economic, cultural, and environmental benefits. Yet some public officials think a battlefield has little value because it is undeveloped land. They assume that preserved battlefields will impede opportunities for development, block potential increases in property values, and thereby slow the flow of revenue to public coffers. The facts show otherwise.

Broadening the tax base does not always mean that real estate taxes will go down. They may go up, depending on how the tax base is broadened, the increase in population, and the extent of new home construction.

The National Park Service (NPS) manages most of the protected battlefields.[1] Those protected by state and municipal agencies and nonprofit organizations have limited data on visitors and their expenditures. Thus, most of the data cited in this handbook are on NPS battlefields. A Civil War battlefield, however, need not be part of the NPS to be a significant historic place or an economic generator. The expansion of protection and interpretation at the state battlefields in Port Hudson, Louisiana, and Perryville, Kentucky, for example, will enhance their roles in both national history and the local economy.

Gettysburg, Pennsylvania, has built an economy based on agriculture and tourism associated with the

1

Gettysburg National Military Park. Visitors spent an estimated $44.5 million there in 1987 (the most recent available data).[2] In 1992 more than 1.2 million people visited the park, and nearly half of them stayed overnight in the Gettysburg area. Visitors in 1992 to the Chickamauga-Chattanooga battlefields in Tennessee numbered 995,600, while Pea Ridge in rural Arkansas had 113,700 visitors.

There has been a steady four percent per year increase in the number of visitors to NPS Civil War sites during the last 10 years and a 20 percent increase in the number of hours visitors stayed at the sites.[3] The number of visitors to state-owned battlefields in 1992 follow:

Prairie Grove, Arkansas, 343,926[4]
Perryville, Kentucky[5], 265,970
Bentonville, North Carolina[6], 22,735
Port Hudson, Louisiana[7], 16,781

Civil War battlefields open to the public draw visitors interested in our nation's history. Their expenditures enrich the local economy.

Battlefields can contribute to the economic well-being—the sustainability —of local communities in several ways:

1. As an income generator, a battlefield attracts direct infusions of wealth from tourism and the park's management expenditures, both of which create jobs in the community. Additional economic benefits flow from sales tax revenue on visitors' purchases.
2. As historic open space, a battlefield adds economic value to adjacent properties and enhances a community's quality of life by protecting its natural resources, environmental qualities, and visual amenities.
3. As a fiscal asset, a battlefield requires few capital expenditures and services by the community unless it is owned and supported by the community.

Some types of development can cost more than they generate in tax dollars because they require public facilities and services (such as schools and roads). A better strategy is for a community to plan for both battlefield preservation and development.

•••

Our battlefield preservation efforts are a key part of our tourism and economic development program, which translates into jobs and a better life for all of us.   *The Hon. Brereton C. Jones*
Governor of Kentucky, Frankfort, Kentucky

Battlefields as Income Generators

Battlefields protected from development and open to the public function just like other basic industries that many communities seek to attract as mainstays of economic development: they draw dollars from outside the community to be spent in the community. Unlike other industries, they are a permanent asset. They don't move, and they don't shut down because they use up natural resources. Even privately owned battlefields can be appreciated from public roads.

In 1992 more than 10 million people visited battlefields. Historic sites in general are increasingly popular tourist attractions. In 1991 more than 84 million people visited the NPS's history-related sites. A 1988 survey of travelers over 50 years of age by the National Tour Association indicated that more than half favored trips to historic sites over other destinations.[8] In state after state, tourists visiting historic sites are likely to stay longer and spend more money than they would for many other types of tourist activities. A 1991 survey of visitors to historic Petersburg, Virginia (including the battlefield), revealed that 82 percent were college educated, 42 percent had an earned income of $50,000 or more, and 79 percent were accompanied by from one to three other visitors[9].

The following figures for Cobb County, Georgia, which includes a Civil War battlefield, show the economic benefits of tourism[10]:

Visitor expenditures in Cobb County, 1991 .... $871 million	
Number of visitors to Kennesaw Mountain Battlefield, 1992 787,400	
Number of travel-related jobs, 1991 22,700	
Travel-related employment payroll, 1991 .... $380 million	
Local tax receipts, 1991 .... $34 million	

Although figures are not available to show the economic value that results specifically from visitors to the battlefield, two points can be highlighted. First, tourism is a major industry for the county, creating more than 22,700 jobs for local citizens. Second, tourism also generates impressive local tax revenue, broadening the tax base beyond real estate taxes.

A look at the total market for tourism in the United States reveals some powerful facts:

- Tourism accounts for $325 billion in annual spending and is the second largest retailing industry in the United States after grocery stores and supermarkets.
- Every $1.00 spent for tourism generates about $3.25 in additional business.
- Approximately 5.4 million people, or more than five percent of the nation's employment base, work in travel-related jobs.
- Travel-related jobs generate about $50 billion in wages and salaries and $25 billion in taxes.[11]

The lesson of these statistics is clear: the business of tourism creates jobs and is a major force in the economies of many communities.

Tourism can be a significant economic force in communities where Civil War battlefields are protected and open to visitors.

Battlefield tourism creates jobs and other economic benefits through

- Expenditures by public agencies for land acquisition, management, and maintenance of battlefields open to visitors
- Expenditures by tourists for lodging, meals, and other travel-related products, sales, and services
- Expenditures by travel-related businesses and their employees for secondary or indirect goods and services
- Tax revenue generated by taxes on purchases by visitors and on services to visitors, such as hotel and restaurant taxes; income taxes from businesses and employees serving visitors; and real estate taxes on land with increased value because it is adjacent to a battlefield

Studies show that a community can realize economic benefits from a protected battlefield. The following discussion examines these benefits.

•••

Heritage Tourism creates new economic development opportunities for communities using their existing historic resources. It is critical that we include tourism in our business development and comprehensive planning efforts. Once our historic landscapes and sites are lost, they cannot be reclaimed to enhance the quality of life and the individuality of an area.

David L. Morgan
State Historic Preservation Officer and Director, Kentucky Heritage Council

Public Agency Expenditures in Communities

Battlefields preserved by federal and state agencies bring significant revenue to surrounding communities.

- Local landowners can benefit from selling their land to a public agency. Federal agencies are required by law to offer fair-market value for properties. The value of land is determined by the local government's comprehensive plan and zoning decisions as well as the market value of comparable properties.
- Construction of park facilities, including visitor centers, roads, parking lots, and other improvements, is usually contracted with local businesses and provides jobs for area residents.
- Battlefield operating funds are spent in the community. Salaries and wages are paid to employees, most of whom are local residents. Supplies and services such as maintenance of buildings and grounds are usually purchased from local businesses.

NPS-managed parks direct substantial funds into local economies, year after year. In 1993 the NPS spent $3.3 million for park management at Gettysburg. The Fredericksburg and Spotsylvania National Military Park spent $1.8 million there in 1991 and increased its budget to $2.8 million in 1993[12]. (see Table 1)

Although budgets for state-owned battlefields are often smaller than NPS budgets, they have a positive economic impact on a community. Table 2 shows the annual budgets for four state-owned battlefields.

TABLE 1: BUDGETED EXPENDITURES FOR OTHER CIVIL WAR PARKS IN 1993	
Petersburg	$1,561,416
Chickamauga	$1,554,900
Vicksburg	$1,500,000
Manassas	$1,040,900
Richmond	$958,800
Wilson's Creek	$831,000
Kennesaw Mountain	$792,500
Shiloh	$760,800
Pea Ridge	$464,000

TABLE 2: STATE-OWNED BATTLEFIELD BUDGETS	
Battlefield	**1992 Budget**
Perryville, Ky.[13]	$119,375
Bentonville, N.C.[14]	154,683
Port Hudson, La.[15]	179,716
Prairie Grove, Ark.[16]	178,525

Visitor Expenditures

Visitors to battlefields purchase merchandise and services, including food, tickets to cultural events and attractions, and overnight lodging. Such expenditures can add millions of dollars to a community's economy. (The NPS does not regularly collect data on how much visitors to parks spend in nearby communities; individual parks that do collect such data find they are useful to the park and the community.)

A 1987 study estimated that visitors to the Gettysburg battlefield spent a total of $44.5 million a year.[17] Visitors to the Pea Ridge National Military Park in Arkansas (a three-hour drive north of Little Rock) spent $10.8 million in 1991.[18] Visitors to Fredericksburg (a one-hour drive south of Washington, D.C.) spent $29.1 million in 1990.[19] Based on the average expenditure per visitor,

Petersburg historic-area visitors spent about $14 million in 1989.[20] The impact of visitor spending at Prairie Grove, Arkansas (a state-owned battlefield park), in 1992 was $4.6 million for in-state visitors and $5 million for out-of-state.[21]

The amount of visitor spending depends on the size of the battlefield (large ones encourage longer visits), the length of visitor stays, how well it and its historic setting have been preserved, the size of the surrounding community, and the linkage of the battlefield to other historic or scenic attractions. Accordingly, spending estimates vary. Day visitors (those who do not stay overnight) spent an average of $17 at Gettysburg (1986)[22], $14 at Harpers Ferry (1987)[23], and $12 at Petersburg, including the Petersburg National Battlefield (1989)[24]. Overnight visitors, who pay for lodging and additional meals, spend considerably more. For example, visitors staying one night in Gettysburg spent an average of $47 per person per day in 1986.[25]

Most estimates of visitor spending count both day and overnight visitors and average their expenditures. The average for all visitors to Gettysburg was $30 in 1986[26]; Petersburg, $56 in 1989[27]; and Wilson's Creek, $49 in 1992.[28] These visitor expenditures, when multiplied by the number of visitors to each Civil War battlefield, are a major force in the local economy.

In addition, visitor spending translates into a substantial number of jobs. Based on employment ratios provided by the U.S. Travel Data Center, for example, it is estimated that tourists to Gettysburg in the late 1980s supported private-sector jobs paying $9.6 million in wages and salaries.[29] A recent study of the Fredericksburg historic district estimated that visitor spending generated 239 full-time equivalent private-sector jobs.[30]

The kinds of jobs created by tourism depend on the resources, vision, and energy of the community. Such jobs include those in motels, restaurants, museums, theaters, and local guide associations. Tourism can spark entrepreneurial opportunities for small businesses, such as bed-and-breakfast inns, antique shops, and craft stores. It can create part-time work for retirees and those seeking a second source of income. Charleston, South Carolina, is a stunning example of a community that has flourished from the benefits of tourism. What began a generation ago as an effort by a few citizens determined to save the town's elegant buildings has become today one of the most vibrant and appealing urban areas in America, enhanced now by the Spoleto Arts Festival.

•••

This handbook is comprehensive and well written. I believe it will save many hours of research by having the information readily available.

William E. Bolte
Commissioner of the Revenue (Retired), Dinwiddie County, Virginia

Secondary Expenditures

The economic benefits of direct spending by battlefield management and visitors are significantly enhanced when the *multiplier effect* is added. In the words of one analyst, "Those dollars live on." Business income from sales to visitors is multiplied when those businesses buy goods and services from other local firms, which in turn make purchases from others.

Depending on the extent to which local businesses can capture secondary spending, the impact of this "ripple effect" on local economies can leverage basic expenditures two to three times. Communities that plan for retaining secondary expenditures through tourism and economic development programs—for example, those that encourage attractive inns, restaurants, and stores in historic buildings near battlefields and in traditional town centers—tend to have higher multipliers than isolated or rural communities, where more dollars from battlefield activities are spent outside the local area.

Communities with a downtown visitor center that complements and enhances the battlefield will also encourage the business community's support of the battlefield. Gettysburg is developing a historic pathway between the battlefield and the town center because a recent study revealed that only 33,000 of the 1.5 million visitors to the battlefield went to downtown Gettysburg and patronized its businesses. The Gettysburg Historic Pathway Plan is designed to encourage more visitors to include the historic downtown in their visit to the park.[31]

Economists estimate multiplier effects in various ways. Total spending usually is determined by using multipliers approximately two times the original direct expenditures. This assumes that some spending "leaks out" to other areas and some multiplies yet again within the community. Using that assumption, indirect spending frequently is estimated to be about equal to direct spending, resulting in a total twice as great as the original direct expenditures. The NPS's "Money Generation Model" manual suggests an average multiplier of 2.0 within a range of 1.2 to 2.8.[32] This model provides a methodology for estimating potential economic benefits.[33] A Pea Ridge (Ark.) study, for example, estimated a multiplier effect of 1.86 on visitor spending, which raised 1991 direct expenditures of $10.8 million to a total estimated economic effect from visitor spending of $20.2 million.[34]

The total economic effect of battlefield expenditures includes direct spending by the public agency managing the battlefield, tourist expenditures, and secondary or indirect expenditures. Consider these 1986 figures for Gettysburg:

1. Battlefield management and maintenance	$ 2.5 million
2. Income from sales to tourists	$44.5 million
3. Secondary income (equal to total of one and two above)	$47 million
Total economic benefits from the battlefield	**$94 million**

(Note that in 1993 the park's budget for Gettysburg increased to $3.3 million, raising total expenditures by at least $6.6 million.)

Tax Revenue

Visitors' dollars can also generate significant revenue through taxes and fees. The U.S. Travel Data Center, for example, estimates that every dollar of business sales to visitors generates 7.3 cents in state and local tax revenue. A study of Fredericksburg's historic district estimated that tourist sales of $53 million per year (including the multiplier effect) yielded an estimated $893,000 in restaurant, lodging, and business license taxes (this total does not include business property taxes and employee income taxes).[35] Local governments also receive payments from the federal government in lieu of property taxes on NPS battlefields. Gettysburg, for example, has received $74,230 from the federal government over the last 10 years in lieu of property taxes.[36]

In summary, sales to visitors support businesses and provide jobs for employees whose incomes flow back into the community in the form of purchases of local goods and services. This flow of economic wealth is taxed in various ways, generating revenue for local governments.

tourist visits
▼
tourist spending
▼
increase in sales of goods and services
▼
more jobs and growth of local businesses
▼
greater business and employee income
▼
increase in spending in community
▼
increase in tax revenue from retail sales

The stream of sales and income means that tourist-related spending is multiplied two to three times, providing jobs for employees in related businesses and services. This ripple effect spreads income derived from battlefield activities throughout the community.

Battlefields as Historic Open Space Assets

In addition to income generated by visitors, battlefields contribute real value to a community as open space: woodlands, riparian habitat, farmlands, and wetlands.

Protected battlefields provide educational, environmental, and economic benefits for their communities.

Amenity Value

The farmlands, meadows, woods, and wetlands on protected battlefields provide green space for the surrounding communities. They not only make the community more attractive but also serve as wonderful outdoor classrooms, providing educational opportunities for residents.

Economic Value

Preservation of open space adds value to adjacent properties. For example, land next to a golf course is more valuable than land a block away. New York City's Central Park is an urban example of the same principle. In the 1850s Frederick Law Olmsted justified the park's economic value by showing that adjacent properties were generating higher tax revenue. Almost 150 years later, a 1991 study found that Central Park has elevated property values within three blocks of the park by $3.2 billion.[37]

A Scenic America publication cites studies measuring the value of open space in both urban and rural areas:

- A public greenbelt in Boulder, Colorado, increased property values in adjacent neighborhoods by $5.4 million. Housing prices decreased by $4.20 for each foot of distance from the greenbelt.
- An analysis of property sales near the 1,294-acre Pennypack Park in Philadelphia showed that the park accounted for 33 percent of the land value 40 feet from the park, nine percent of land value at 1,000 feet from the park, and 4.2 percent at 2,500 feet from the park.
- In Dayton, Ohio, the prices of homes adjacent to an arboretum averaged five percent higher than those nearby.
- Land adjoining farmland zoned exclusively for agricultural use in Salem, Oregon, was worth $1,200 more per acre than land 1,000 feet away from the farmland.[38]

Battlefields can provide important open space amenities for nearby residents, especially in urban or developing areas, and, by increasing property values, these amenities can translate into economic benefits for adjacent property owners.

A community, however, must plan carefully for the use of the land adjacent to its battlefield so that the use does not detract from the battlefield setting or the community's other assets. For example, Gettysburg permitted development of stores, motels, and fast-food chains along the road across from the park. Such development detracts from the solemnity of the battlefield and decreases the volume of business in the historic town center.

•••

This handbook emphasizes the need for planning both the battlefield and the surrounding area including the communities where greatest tourism economic impacts will be realized.   *Clare A. Gunn*

Professor Emeritus, Texas A&M University, College Station, Texas

11

Battlefields as Fiscal Assets

One aspect of the economic value of open land can be measured by comparing the cost of providing public services to it with the ongoing costs of providing services required for developed land. Fiscal impact data demonstrate that open space generates revenue but requires few services.

	EXPENDITURE/REVENUE DATA FOR RESIDENTIAL DEVELOPMENT AND OPEN LANDS	
	Cost of Services per Dollar of Tax Revenue	
Area	**Residential Area**	**Open Land**
Dutchess County, N.Y.[43]	$1.11 - 1.23	$0.17 - 0.74
Culpeper County, Va.[44]	$1.25	$0.19
Rappahannock County, Va.[45]	n.a.	$0.17
Deerfield, Mass.[46]	$1.16	$0.29
Hebron, Conn.[47]	$1.06	$0.36
Beekman, N.Y.[48]	$1.12	$0.48
Straban Township, Adams County, Pa.[49]	$1.10	$0.12

A study of Dutchess County, New York, estimated that public expenditures for services to open lands (farmlands, parks, vacant, wild and forested, and water) required between 17 and 74 cents of each tax dollar collected from landowners.[39] In Culpeper County, Virginia, farm, forest, and open-space lands required only $350,000 in expenditures but returned nearly $1.9 million in revenue to the county, or about 19 cents in expenditures for each dollar in revenue.[40] A similar study of Rappahannock County, Virginia, showed that open lands generated an 83-cent surplus for every dollar their owners paid in taxes.[41] A 1992 study for Straban Township in Adams County, Pennsylvania, concluded that "farm and open land provide clear economic benefits to all residents of the township by providing more in revenue than they require in local expenditures."[42]

Studies such as these can help community leaders calculate the potential benefits of open space for their community and the relationship of open space to developed areas. The fiscal impacts of development in each community depend on how much the budget relies on property taxes compared with other revenue, how much tax revenue new development will net, the ratio of public/private sharing of

12

infrastructure costs for new development, and other details
of the community's fiscal picture. In addition, communities
with tourism potential should consider the one-time effect
of providing jobs through new house construction compared with the ongoing creation of jobs from tourism.

*The cost/revenue comparison between new homes
and open lands shows that, in most jurisdictions, new
houses are fiscal burdens (i.e., pay less in taxes than they
cost in services) whereas open lands provide fiscal surpluses (i.e., pay more in taxes than they cost in services).*

The data from Massachusetts, New York, Connecticut,
Virginia, and Maine show that a Civil War battlefield—preserved through some form of private open use, such as agriculture—can continue to generate fiscal surpluses to the
community even though it does not provide the added economic benefits of tourism. This evidence also suggests that it is
important for community leaders to compute two costs to the
community over a period of 20 years or so: (1) the cost of purchasing a battlefield either in fee or easement and preserving it
as open space, and (2) the cost of permitting development on it.
    Protected battlefields that are open to the public can
yield a fiscal surplus to a community even though they are off
the tax rolls. The size of the surplus will depend on the size,
facilities, and location of the battlefield, as well as which public agency or nonprofit organization pays the capital and operating costs. For example, city- or county-owned battlefields
can be an asset even though they must be supported by local
tax revenue. An increase in the number of visitors may require improvements to local roads and highways, which often
are funded in part by state governments. Water supply and
sewage disposal usually are furnished by the park's on-site facilities. Battlefields require minimal police and fire protection
from the community, and they do not generate demands for
schools or other administrative and social services.
    In summary, Civil War battlefields that are protected
and open to the public can offer net economic benefits to a
community: they generate income for community businesses and residents and generate sales and real estate tax
revenue. They also provide attractive open space and enhance the community's character and cultural life.

13

How Residential, Commercial, and Industrial Development of Battlefields Can Cost Taxpayers

Many battlefields and their settings are still privately owned. When development opportunities arise, private owners of battlefield properties often want to capitalize on the increasing value of their properties. Public officials frequently support such opportunities. Why? Public officials assume that real estate development will *always* benefit the community and, by broadening the tax base, will decrease the taxpayers' burdens more than a protected battlefield.

These assumptions are often wrong. Why? Because the *costs of development* to local governments often are misunderstood and underestimated. The fiscal benefits of development as revenue generators for local governments frequently are a mirage. The stimulus provided by new-house construction is followed by increased costs of services. Local governments often must spend more for services and infrastructure to support new development than they get back in tax revenue. Residents' taxes then go up. Especially in rural areas, large-scale development can produce serious financial problems for local public officials and can result in higher property taxes for everyone. By contrast, as already discussed, protected battlefields require few services from local governments and can be fiscal assets.

Communities can enjoy the benefits of both battlefields and development by encouraging well-planned development away from, rather than on, battlefields. This strategy takes full advantage of both battlefield preservation and development to improve the fiscal condition of local governments.

Many communities can benefit from development. However, the real estate tax rate and the effects of development on the quality of life for residents depend on how, where, when, and what kind of development occurs. A report on the relationship of the tax base to the tax bill in Vermont observed the following:

While local officials may be considering the tax consequences of new development, some Vermonters are complaining of ugly strip developments and inappropriate land use decisions, which they attribute to the quest for tax base. After listening to Vermonters across the state, the Governor's Commission on Vermont's Future summarized their impressions this way: "Most towns, confronted with the rising cost of services, compete for development to increase their tax base. This competition conflicts with the planning process. Towns are forced to waive zoning requirements, make improper siting decisions, and, in general, pursue short-term objectives at the expense of long-term goals.[50]

Development can bring its own problems:

- Development can require extensive—and expensive— improvements in communities that have modest levels of public facilities (such as roads, schools, and utilities). Many of these improvements must be financed by taxes imposed by local governments.
- Some types of residential development commonly generate much less in taxes and other revenue than the costs of public services they demand. They produce fiscal deficits rather than surpluses and result in higher property taxes for current residents.
- Even development that generates more revenue than costs (such as commercial and industrial projects) can stimulate additional development (such as more houses), which can have a negative fiscal impact. Such development produces either a net loss to local government or higher real estate taxes than those in effect before the new development.
- New development can change the character of a community. New development need not be ugly or destroy "main street" or the countryside, but too often it does. Of course, tourism can, and often does, change a community's character. However, it does not have to result in ugly strip development, particularly along the boundaries of battlefields that are open to visitors. Amenities for visitors—when carefully considered by local leaders—can enhance the community's character. One fine example is the historic town of Sharpsburg, Maryland, near the Antietam battlefield.

Here is the evidence.

Development Requires Expensive Infrastructure

Development that converts woodlands and farmlands to residential housing will require extensive construction of roads, utilities, and schools. Much of the burden of capital and operating costs for expanded public facilities frequently is borne by all taxpayers in the jurisdiction. Development will also affect facilities in nearby jurisdictions; police and fire departments' budgets will increase. Local governments unaccustomed to development can be unprepared to evaluate either the needs or the impacts of new development. They can be surprised a few years later by the real costs, a budget deficit, and the ire of taxpayers when taxes are increased to pay for development.

Local governments with experience in regulating development often impose impact fees or require developers to build or assist in funding facilities. Even then, it is difficult for many local governments to maintain adequate services and infrastructure—for evidence, one need only read the newspaper stories about traffic congestion and school budget problems in any rapidly growing area. It is not surprising, then, that local governments, particularly those inexperienced in regulating development and those with limited regulatory powers (such as Virginia localities), risk financial difficulties by promoting development of open land.

Development-related costs can be substantial. The rural farming community of Tracy, California, for example, tried to plan carefully for the roads, drainage, parks, and other facilities needed for development of as many as 8,800 housing units. The estimated improvement costs came to $147 million, or an average of $16,700 per housing unit.[51] These costs may be borne by the entire community or shared among the developers, the users, and the public. Tracy officials worked out a cost-sharing program to pay for the improvements without affecting tax rates of existing residents.

Improvement costs in other communities could be higher or lower than those in Tracy, depending on local standards and construction costs. For example, estimated costs of improvements in Culpeper County were $5,566 per unit.[52] The potential total impact of such costs depends on whether there are dozens or hundreds of proposed new housing units. How much will be paid by existing taxpayers depends on the determination of voters and local officials to enact regulations to shift costs to the new development rather than existing property owners—and the legal authority to do so.

Experience shows that rural communities frequently are heavily impacted by the costs of providing public facilities for new development: homeowners' taxes go up.

Broadening the Tax Base
Can Generate Fiscal Deficits

Public officials often seek new development to expand community tax bases and garner new revenue for public coffers. New homes, shopping centers, and industrial parks may pay property, income, sales, and excise taxes, as well as various fees for services. These potential revenues promise to improve local fiscal conditions.

The problem is that some development, especially residential, usually does not generate enough revenue to cover the full cost of the public services it requires. Many local governments do not require homeowners to pay enough in taxes to cover the cost of services, relying instead on commercial and industrial development to pay a large share of the taxes. Tax revenue will be further decreased if the town offers real estate tax breaks to attract industrial and commercial development.

In many communities, experience has shown that under current tax systems new homes do not pay their own way until the value of the house reaches $300,000 or more. A study by the Piedmont Environmental Council, for example, found that a new house in Culpeper County would have to be valued at $304,000 to generate enough tax revenue to offset its service costs.[53] In Spotsylvania County, that figure soars to between $400,000 and $500,000 for a family with two school-age children.[54] Expenditures for public schools generally account for 50 to 70 percent of all local expenditures. Moderately priced homes for families that include school-age children usually pay only part of their share of public expenditures. Taxes on other types of development and on agricultural land make up the balance.

17

Studies have documented the fiscal shortfall created by residential development. In Dutchess County, New York, the cost of servicing residential development ranged from $1.11 to $1.23 for every dollar of revenue generated by housing units.[55] In Otsego Township, Wright County, Minnesota, each home would cost the township $142.00 a year in services but would generate only $128.40 a year in revenue, almost a 10 percent shortfall each year.[56] In Culpeper County, an analysis estimated that an average new residential unit would require annual county expenditures of $2,167 but would only generate annual revenue of about $1,738.[57]

Local governments find that revenue from new home development rarely catches up with demands for new facilities and services. In response, public officials raise taxes to increase the revenue stream; the new rates apply to older properties as well as to new ones. Residents then see their taxes increased by the new development that was supposed to broaden the tax base and, thereby, lower their taxes.

•••

The *Dollar$ and Sense of Battlefield Preservation* does make a compelling case for the economic values of protected battlefields.

T. H. Kendall, III
Landowner and business executive, Bolton, Mississippi

Commercial and Industrial Development Generate Hidden Costs

Commercial and industrial development often appear attractive to local public officials because they produce substantial tax revenue, usually well above their direct costs for public services. Compared with revenue from nonresidential development, the tax yield from battlefield sites appears relatively insignificant. But there is an offsetting factor. Commercial and industrial development can stimulate other development that ultimately will escalate public costs, causing local governments to raise taxes to cope with them. The experiences of Culpeper and Albemarle counties in Virginia and the town of Monkton, Vermont, are worth noting.

A fiscal analysis of a proposed industrial park on the site of the Brandy Station battlefield in Culpeper County

18

estimated the park would employ about 8,595 workers and generate another 33,000 jobs within the county. Since the county has few unemployed workers, most of the workers would have to be recruited from outside the county. The study determined that new jobs would expand housing production in the county, driving up its population from the present 26,200 to 97,091 within 20 years. Moreover, county expenditures for facilities and services to meet the new housing demand would rise by 470 percent while revenue would increase by only 449 percent, resulting in a revenue shortfall of $71.1 million over 20 years. The study concluded that the positive fiscal effect of the industrial park would be more than offset by the negative impact of residential services required by the new employees.[58]

Such studies are controversial; experts disagree about methods of projecting costs and revenue. The Culpeper study, for example, may have underestimated the probable tax base increases that would result from new development and overestimated the amount of new housing development. Fiscal studies include many arguable assumptions and estimates of future trends. In addition, county officials could take steps to reduce the public costs of development. The Culpeper County study, nevertheless, does show that the proposed industrial development would have a significant impact on the county's future fiscal condition.

A study of the economic effects of a proposed three-million-square-foot research park in Albemarle County showed results similar to those in the Culpeper study. The Piedmont Environmental Council's study concluded that significant new residential costs would accompany the growth in population stimulated by this new employer and would create a substantial deficit for the county. Offsetting this deficit could cost the owner of an average $120,000 home an additional $480 in real estate taxes. "Population growth and residential development are not inevitable, but responsive to other forces, primarily growth of the employment base. In a low unemployment economy such as Albemarle's, it is growth in the industrial and commercial sectors of the economy which stimulates growth in the residential sector." Between 1979 and 1988, the population grew 18 percent (10,000) and county real estate taxes increased 78 percent, even though the real estate tax base expanded by 44 percent (nearly $499 million). The broadening of the real estate tax base did not lower residents' real estate taxes.[59]

In states such as Vermont, which provide school aid to towns according to a formula, school funding is reduced as local tax revenue increases. In Monkton, a proposed commercial development would have increased real estate tax revenue. However, the increase in local tax revenue would trigger a decrease in state funds for Monkton's schools. The real estate tax, therefore, could be reduced by only 0.5 cents because real estate taxes would have to pay for a higher percentage of public school costs. When the town officials added the costs of municipal services, they concluded that the new development would raise, not lower, property taxes.[60]

Community leaders need data that can inform their critical decisions about development and battlefield preservation and how both will affect the community's fiscal circumstance. Those data in combination with broad public involvement in the development of the community's vision of its future will help leaders make wise decisions about preservation and development.

●●●

Long term versus short term economic returns through preservation of our cultural and natural resources generate long term quality economic growth which will reap many times the returns of the "quick, cheap, and easy" development. *Gordon Echols*
Professor, Texas A&M University College of Architecture
College Station, Texas

Development Changes a Community's Character

Development can cause irreversible changes in the character of a community—and in its cost of living. Community leaders must plan for controlling the location, amount, and quality of growth, or they will discover that the assumption that "more development is better" is untrue. Strip shopping centers hurt retail businesses in traditional town centers, leaving them decrepit, devalued, and deserted. Commercial strips line highways with the signs of nationally franchised businesses, making one town look like the next. Tract housing replaces open farmlands and multiplies the costs of services, often changing open land that generated a net surplus in taxes into developed land that generates losses. New industries pop up in the countryside, creating traffic congestion.

Less visibly, development inevitably changes living conditions for longtime residents. As roads, schools, and other public facilities become overloaded, costly new ones must be built—usually with revenue from higher real estate taxes on all houses. New homes establish new price levels, causing the value of older homes to rise, along with property taxes. Older people with fixed incomes find it increasingly expensive to continue living in their homes, as will the sons and daughters of longtime residents who need affordable housing both to rent and buy. These are major problems in many small towns and rural communities affected by development.

Increasingly, local governments are taking early action to regain or retain local control: if a community does not decide through its comprehensive plan what it wants to be, outside forces, such as fast-food chains and motels, will decide. Communities are providing variety in housing and acting to preserve their historic and scenic areas and their precious water supplies.

A community that comes together to create a vision of its future can then be guided by that vision to preserve its character and quality of life.

By planning ahead, creating partnerships, and involving the entire community, leaders can help preserve the character of their community.

•••

A community with a Civil War battlefield is unique. That's when history and events, the heritage of an area, become an asset, a base for local character that sets an area apart. Now that we are in a world where maintaining an economy is as hard as growing one, finding an asset—like an area's Civil War heritage—is important. Building on such real themes, as opposed to the commercial 'theme parks,' has benefit because it is unique.

It is my belief that once the "heritage theme" is embraced by a community, it is owned by the citizens; then the investment in preservation actions will follow.   *Thomas J. Christoffel*
Executive Director, Lord Fairfax Planning District Commission
Front Royal, Virginia

A Better Strategy:
Battlefield Preservation AND Development

It is often possible for local governments to enjoy the fruits of carefully considered new development and to reap the economic benefits of preserving Civil War battlefields. The issues to be resolved are

- where a community encourages development
- how a community preserves its battlefield within a comprehensive plan that implements the community's vision for its future
- how a community plans for its sustainability through diversification

A protected battlefield can be a dynamic partner with both residential and nonresidential development. The balance between preservation and development requires planning: creating an economic development policy that builds on community strengths, one of which is the protected battlefield. Planning must involve the community and then be honored by those authorized to enact the plan through zoning and other governmental actions.

•••

As agriculture and heavy industry, traditional economic sources for smaller rural communitites, continue to shrink, new funding sources are sought. A rural battlefield site provides an excellent economic option in an overall diverse development plan.   *Alton Kelley*

Executive Director, Maury County Convention and Visitors Bureau

Columbia, Tennessee

The Advantages of Community Planning and Partnerships

The cooperative effort at Antietam National Battlefield in Maryland illustrates one community's commitment to protect its heritage. (See Appendix C) Congress created the Antietam National Battlefield in 1890 by protecting a few acres and some roads that were important to teaching military tactics, while leaving the remaining agricultural land unprotected. Since then, the park boundary has been expanded to include 3,250 of the approximately 8,000 acres of the historic battlefield. About 10 years ago Washington County, in response to the citizens of the Sharpsburg area, decided to preserve the historic integrity of the town by zoning it entirely for residential use. In addition, the state has an active program for purchasing easements and has committed $3 million in ISTEA transportation enhancement funds and $3 million in state Program Open Space funds to protect more than 2,500 acres of farmland surrounding the Antietam battlefield. In 1990 Washington County officials approved the Antietam historic overlay zoning to ensure that future development is compatible with the historic quality of the area, requiring design review of new structures.[61]

The public and the private sectors are working to implement plans to protect Antietam's heritage. The Richard King Mellon Foundation acquired and donated the Cornfield and West Woods as additions to Antietam. At nearby Grove Farm (where President Lincoln met with U.S. generals after the battle), 40 acres are protected through a partnership of the Save Historic Antietam Foundation (SHAF), the Maryland Environmental Trust, the Civil War Trust, and the Association for the Preservation of Civil War Sites. Another five acres of Grove Farm were protected through the joint efforts of Maryland's Department of Transportation, using ISTEA funds, SHAF, and The Conservation Fund. Twenty acres of commercially zoned land at Grove Farm were purchased, along with a conservation easement on the remaining 30 acres of the farm and the historic Mount Airy mansion and buildings, using funds from the Department of Natural Resources' Program Open Space and ISTEA. These acquisitions, and an easement purchased over the 256-acre Coffman farm north of the battlefield, represent the first steps in a comprehensive strategy developed by the Governor's Civil War Heritage Commission. This effort will preserve more than 800 acres of land to protect views of and approaches to the Antietam battlefield.

Another example of the benefits of planning and partnership can be found in Perryville, Kentucky. The Perryville Enhancement Project—the dynamic partnership that includes the Perryville Battlefield Commission, the Kentucky Heritage Council, the Perryville Battlefield Preservation Association, the city of Perryville, the state of Kentucky, Boyle County, and the National Park Service—is working together with The Conservation Fund to preserve the 19th century significance of the community and its battlefield, led by Governor Brereton Jones's commitment of $2.5 million in ISTEA funds.

Partners in battlefield protection, such as those in Maryland and Kentucky, have a stewardship opportunity and an obligation to plan for and manage tourism so that the battlefield continues to be a priceless treasure for visitors today and in the future.

Community Interests vs. Private Interests

One of the most difficult problems public officials face in deciding to preserve battlefields is how to balance national, community, and private interests. Property owners frequently stand to gain large profits from zoning changes that would enable them to sell their land for development. A local jurisdiction could benefit more from preserving the battlefield and planning development elsewhere. Public officials often are reluctant to deny landowners the opportunities for profits, even if those profits will result in development that will impact other landowners and destroy a nationally significant historic area.

The future of a community is determined largely by those who make its planning and zoning decisions. Those decisions merit community-wide deliberation, examining the effect on its economy and the significance of its heritage. When the stakes are clear, many public officials decide in favor of battlefield preservation. Some do not.

The uncertain future of the battlefield at Brandy Station, site of the largest cavalry battle fought in North America, illustrates the problems in balancing national, local, and private interests. The battlefield remained essentially as it was in 1863, rural Virginia farmland, until a developer assembled thousands of acres, including much of the battlefield, for residential and industrial development. The Culpeper County Board of Supervisors rejected the county planning board's preservation plan, which recognized the importance of the battlefield, and changed the zoning to permit industrial development on the battlefield. Citizens from the county and across the nation pressed for designation of the battlefield as a state historic landmark, and the National Park Service declared it eligible for the National Register of Historic Places. In 1992 Secretary of the Interior Manuel Lujan removed the property from eligibility for the National Register, and a local citizen's group lost its lawsuit against the county to reverse the zoning change.

If the Brandy Station battlefield were protected and
open to the public, it could enhance the character of the
community and produce economic benefits for the county.
Industrial development on the battlefield would obliterate
this possibility. Preserving the battlefield while developing
the industrial area at a nearby site could provide two
sources of economic benefit to the county: tourism and an
industrial park.

•••

I think this will be an extremely valuable tool for community leaders and should help dispel the myths about the incompatibility of land
conservation and economic development.   *Henry A. Jordan, M.D.*
Chairman, The Countryside Institute, Plymouth Meeting, Pennsylvania

The U.S. Constitution and Battlefield Preservation

The Fifth Amendment to the Constitution provides
that private property shall not "be taken for public use
without just compensation." In the 1978 *Penn Central*
case, the Supreme Court ruled that municipal landmarks
ordinances are constitutional, and that an ordinance deny-
ing a landowner maximum profit from the property is not
an unconstitutional taking, if the owner retains a reasonable economic use of the property.

Local governments in all states possess a considerable amount of legal power to regulate the use of privately held land without compensating landowners. The
range of that power varies from state to state and is
guarded by many technical requirements. But generally,
if public officials determine that important public interests are at stake, if they undertake competent studies to
provide the basis for regulations, and if they adopt regulations according to reasonable due process procedures, local governments can exercise strong control over use of
private land, including prohibiting further development
or changes in use.

Public officials are well aware that although property
owners may be for government actions that increase the
monetary value of their properties—such as prohibiting a
waste dump next door or extending water and sewer
lines—they may be against government actions, such as

zoning changes, that would lower the potential for increase in the value of their land. Officials must weigh the
future possibility of economic benefits for one landowner
against the potential liabilities for others (as well as for future generations), such as threats to public health and
safety, the environment, and historic places. Robert E.
Stipe, a national authority on preservation, summarized
the challenges: "For preservation to succeed at the turn of
the century absolutely requires more extensive, more serious, more constructive, and generally better local government participation in the preservation process than we
have had up till now."[62]

In 1993 the National Trust for Historic Preservation
devoted an issue of the journal *Forum* to property rights,
with the goal, as stated by David A. Doheny, the Trust's
general counsel, of contributing "to a better understanding
of how to balance the vital and often conflicting considerations of private property rights and common benefits and
responsibilities." Excerpts from these essays are included
in this handbook to foster that understanding as it relates
to battlefield preservation (see appendix D).[63] These three
essays, each of which is written by a nationally recognized
authority on historic preservation, present ideas that can
be useful to community leaders who want to realize the
potential economic benefits from protecting their battlefields. Their decisions regarding comprehensive plans,
zoning, and preservation ordinances will affect battlefield
preservation and have economic implications for all landowners. These ideas also can help officials ensure the fair-
ness and constitutionality of their decisions.

Development Can Benefit from Historic Preservation

There are developers who have worked with community leaders and preservationists on developments that are
economic successes because of preservation. For example,
the St. Louis train station, one of America's great buildings, is now restored as a hotel and shops. Other examples
are the historic towns of New Castle, Delaware, and
Charleston, South Carolina.

[1] National Park Service, Civil War Sites Advisory Commission Report (Washington, D.C., 1993). Available from the NPS American Battlefield Protection Program. Of the 50 Priority I battlefields, areas of 22 are in the NPS; lands on eight are state owned; 18 have no protection; two have some land protected by other agencies.

[2] George L. Youngblood, Jerry Bussell, Jesse T. Stacks III, and Gerald R. Wilson, Jr., "The Economic Impact of Tourism, Generated by the Gettysburg National Military Park, on the Economy of Gettysburg" (study sponsored by Gettysburg National Military Park with Shippensburg State College, 1987). It should be noted that this study computes visitor expenditures on pages 39-43 that are considerably lower than those reported on page 51, which are the figures most often cited by later studies. No reasons are given for the difference, and in neither case is a multiplier applied. For the purposes of this study, the spending estimates given on pages 39-43 are used. These are the most recent for Gettysburg.

[3] NPS, *Annual Statistical Abstracts* (prepared by the Socio-Economic Division).

[4] Arkansas Department of Parks and Tourism, Memorandum from the director of state parks, June 25, 1993.

[5] Kentucky Department of Parks, Memorandum, June 1, 1993.

[6] North Carolina Department of Natural Resources, Historic Sites Section, Memorandum, May 26, 1993,

[7] Louisiana Department of Culture, Recreation, and Tourism, Memorandum from the director of state parks, June 25, 1993.

[8] National Tour Association, 1988 survey, cited in "Heritage Tourism Initiative Fact Sheet" (prepared by the National Trust for Historic Preservation).

[9] Christopher R. Hoffner, "Survey of Visitors to Petersburg Tourism Sites" (study prepared for the City of Petersburg Department of Tourism, 1990).

[10] Cobb Historic Tourism study.

[11] Data published by the U.S. Travel Data Center, Washington, D.C.

[12] Questionnaire from The Conservation Fund to NPS superintendents of Civil War battlefields (1992).

[13] Kentucky Department of Parks, Memorandum, June 1, 1993.

[14] North Carolina, Memorandum.

[15] Louisiana, Memorandum.

[16] Arkansas, Memorandum.

[17] Youngblood et al., "Economic Impact . . . on Gettysburg."

[18] Conservation Fund questionnaire (1992).

[19] *The Economic Benefits of Preserving Community Character, A Case Study: Fredericksburg, Virginia* (prepared by the Government Finance Research Center for the National Trust for Historic Preservation and Scenic America).

[20] Hoffner, "Visitors to Petersburg."

[21] Arkansas, Memorandum.

[22] Youngblood et al., "Economic Impact . . . on Gettysburg."

[23] Gary E. Machlis and Margaret Littlejohn, *A Diversity of Factors* (University of Idaho, 1991). This publication also includes per capita expenditures from five additional parks (these include travel, lodging, food, and other): Denali National Park and Preserve, $76; Yellowstone National Park, $51; Muir Woods National Monument, $43; Bryce

27

Canyon National Park, $28; Mesa Verde, $18.
[24] Hoffner, "Visitors to Petersburg."
[25] Youngblood et al., "Economic Impact . . . of Gettysburg."
[26] Ibid.
[27] Hoffner, "Visitors to Petersburg."
[28] Conservation Fund questionnaire (1992).
[29] The U.S. Travel Data Center estimates that business payrolls supported by visitor spending equal 21.6 percent of sales income, and
average wages and salaries equal $9,655. Gettysburg's visitor spending
of $44.5 million yields 995 jobs ($44.5 million multiplied by 21.6
percent), and 995 jobs at $9,655 generates $9.6 million in local
payrolls. This compares to a 1988 study by the Adams County
Economic Development Office, which determined that approximately
1,200 county residents were employed in travel-related jobs. The U.S.
Travel Data Center has published the following figures on the
economic impact of visitors:

**ANNUAL IMPACT OF 100 ADDITIONAL VISITORS A DAY ON THE
AVERAGE U.S. COMMUNITY, 1990 PRELIMINARY**

Direct impact	Total impact*
$1.5 million in retail and service industry sales to visitors	$2.8 million in business receipts
$332,000 in wages and salaries	$768,000 in wages and salaries
29 new travel industry jobs providing additional income for 23 households with 61 residents	67 new jobs providing additional income for 52 households with 141 residents
$116,000 in state and local tax revenue, enough to support 22 school children	$189,000 in state and local tax revenue, enough to support 35 school children
Two or more retail or service establishments	Four more retail or service establishments

includes direct, indirect, and induced impact

---

[30] *Preserving Community Character: Fredericksburg.*
[31] *Gettysburg Historic Pathway Plan.*
[32] NPS, *The Money Generation Model* (prepared by the Socio-Economic
Studies Division, Denver, 1990).
[33] NPS, Memorandum from the assistant to the director for science and
technology, May 26, 1992. The NPS used the Money Generation
Model to calculate the estimated economic effects of visitors to NPS
park units (including historic parks) in the sparsely settled west.
These estimates suggest the substantial economic benefits of tourism.
1. The economic impact in 1990 of visitors to 13 NPS park units in
New Mexico totaled:
  • annual revenue resulting from sales of goods and services in the
  13 local business trading areas: $157,975,000

- state and local tax revenues generated: $10,110,000
- jobs created: 4,740

2. The economic impacts of expenditures by out-of-state visitors to 13 NPS park units in Utah in 1989:
   - annual revenue resulting from sales of goods and services in the 13 local business trading areas: $258,630,000
   - state and local tax revenues generated: $16,550,000
   - jobs created: 5,175

3. The economic impacts of expenditures by nonlocal visitors to 20 NPS park units in Arizona in 1990:
   - annual revenue resulting from sale of goods and services in the 20 local business trading areas: $875,273,000
   - total state sales and income tax revenues generated by nonlocal park visitor expenditures: $54,921,000

[34] Dennis Beckmann and Edward Fryar, "Arkansas Agricultural Econometric Model with Input/Output Analysis" (University, Fayetteville, 1987).

[35] *Preserving Community Character: Fredericksburg.*

[36] "Park Contributes to Local Tax Base," *Gettysburg Quarterly* 1, no. 1 (July 1992).

[37] E. S. Savas, "The Value of Central Park" (manuscript, Baruch College Center for Management, June 1992).

[38] Elizabeth Brabec, "On the Value of Open Spaces," Scenic America Technical Information, vol. 1, no. 2 (Washington, D.C., 1992).

[39] Christopher P. Bucknall, *The Real Cost of Development* (prepared for Scenic Hudson, Inc., Poughkeepsie, 1989).

[40] Arthur B. Larson and Tamara A. Vance, "Fiscal Impacts of Residential Development in Culpeper County, Virginia" (report prepared for the Piedmont Environmental Council, 1988).

[41] Alexander Sharp, "Fiscal Impact of Major Land Uses in Rappahannock County" (prepared for the Rappahannock League for Environmental Protection and the Piedmont Environmental Council, 1991).

[42] Timothy Kelsey, "The Public Finance Implications of Land Uses and Community Services" (Straban Township, Adams County, Pa., 1992).

[43] Bucknall, *Real Cost of Development.*

[44] Letter to The Conservation Fund from the administration of Spotsylvania County (November 1993).

[45] Sharp, "Fiscal Impact . . . in Rappahannock County."

[46] "Making a Positive Contribution," *American Farmland* (Fall 1991).

[47] Ibid.

[48] Ibid.

[49] Kelsey, "Public Finance Implications."

[50] Deborah Brighton, "The Tax Base and the Tax Bill" (prepared for the Vermont League of Cities and Towns and the Vermont Natural Resources Council, 1990).

[51] Douglas R. Porter, "Facing Growth with a Plan: Tracy and Carlsbad, CA," *Urban Land* (June 1992).

[52] Larson and Vance, "Fiscal Impacts . . . in Culpeper County."

[53] Ibid.

[54] Letter from Spotsylvania County (November 1993).

[55] Bucknall, *Real Cost of Development.*

[56] Robert J. Gray and Joanne Dann, "Development in Wright County, The Revenue/Cost Relationship" (1989).

[57] Larson and Vance, "Fiscal Impacts . . . in Culpeper County."

[58] John Petersen and Matthew Montavon, "Elkwood Downs: Its Fiscal Implications for Culpeper County" (prepared for the Friends of Brandy Station, 1990). Available from the National Trust for Historic Preservation.

[59] C. Timothy Lindstrom, "An Analysis of the Fiscal Impact of The University of Virginia Real Estate Foundation's Proposed Research Park" (staff report of the Piedmont Environmental Council, 1989).

[60] Brighton, "Tax Base."

[61] Maryland Land Preservation and Recreation Plan, Maryland Office of Planning (Baltimore, 1993, updated 1994).

[62] Robert E. Stipe, "Preserving Historical and Cultural Landscapes: Some Emerging Issues" (Vincent Lecture, School of Environmental Design, University of Georgia, May 17, 1989).

[63] *Forum* 7, no. 4 (July-August 1993).

Part Two

Developing a Plan for Battlefield Preservation

Once a community decides that its battlefield merits preservation, it should develop a comprehensive preservation plan that is woven together with other community concerns. A good place to begin is with the National Trust's *Saving Place* materials, developed to assist leaders working to protect the character of their communities. While the focus of *Saving Place* is on New England, it is comprehensive and practical enough to be used nationwide. It includes a beautiful and informative video about managing growth, in which the "experts" are community leaders. The accompanying booklet includes a detailed checklist to guide leaders in analyzing the needs, assets, and challenges in preserving community character and integrity.[1]

Preserving a Civil War battlefield requires imagination, cooperation, and planning, but most important, it requires the dedicated efforts of public and private community leaders to create a preservation plan. The following discussion outlines seven important steps in the process.

Know the Battlefield

Understanding the events that took place on the battlefield and knowing the extent and current status of lands involved are the first important steps in developing a preservation strategy. A site analysis should locate the battlefield and show it and its historic buildings clearly on today's maps (including Geographic Information System computer technology, if available). Information on zoning

and current land uses and values is critically important.
The report of the Civil War Sites Advisory Commission
provides much of the information communities will need
about the location of the 384 most significant battlefields.[2]
The Civil War Battlefield Guide contains maps and information on 60 of them.[3] Historians can describe the landscape as it was on the day of the battle. Today's woodlands
may have been fields then, which if restored will help visitors understand the battle. The American Battlefield Protection Program of the NPS provides published materials
and technical assistance to help communities in surveying
and researching battlefield sites.

Involve All Citizens

Preservation will be possible only with broad support
from the community. Early involvement of individual citizens and landowners, public officials and agencies, the
business and education communities, and nonprofit organizations will help a community develop its vision for its
future. After identifying the likely partners in the preservation effort—those who will have a stake in the outcome—
organize a "friends of the park" nonprofit. Prospective
board members include property owners, representatives
of environmental and historic preservation groups, business leaders, educators, and public officials. There are
many ways to attract members, including holding public
meetings, conducting public opinion surveys, and distrib-
uting newsletters and brochures.

Define the Probable Issues

The information about the battlefield will begin to
shape the size, scope, and complexity of the preservation
effort. At this point, it is important to identify the issues
that will need to be resolved.
- Is development in the area proceeding at a pace that
  will soon threaten significant areas of the battlefield?
- What effects will public policies and zoning have on the
  battlefield?
- Is the community guided by a comprehensive plan?
- What does the plan say about preservation?
- Are affected landowners interested in preservation?
- Are public officials aware of the potential for economic

growth through heritage tourism and historic preservation?

- What public agency or nonprofit organization will own and manage the battlefield if it is open to the public?
- How can the community work in partnership with the landowner(s) if the battlefield remains private property?

Build a Strategy

The friends organization, working with other community groups, should construct a preservation strategy that includes:

- The community's vision for its future and the place of the battlefield within that vision
- Development of the plan for the battlefield
- Advice from leaders in other communities who have tackled similar problems
- A thorough analysis—containing as much detail as time and money permit—of the economic feasibility of preservation for both the public and private sectors, including the costs and benefits in tax revenue of both development and preservation on and near the battlefield
- Partnerships among those who can promote success in preserving the battlefield: corporations, landowners, developers, public agencies, foundations, businesses, nonprofits, colleges, schools, and industries that complement the battlefields, including tourism, agriculture, and forestry

The strategy should result in an action agenda that identifies what should be done and when, who should be responsible, what other groups should be involved, and how the effort should be financed. If special legislation will be required to preserve the site, the strategy should include a program to build political support.

Conduct a Fiscal Impact Analysis

The National Trust for Historic Preservation is developing a workbook for community leaders entitled *The Economic and Fiscal Impacts of Preserving Historic Open Spaces*, sponsored by the NPS. Using case studies of Civil War battlefields in Tennessee and Virginia and adapting the techniques of fiscal impact and regional economics, the guide presents methods for examining the financial feasibility of alternative ways of preserving historic open space. It can be used to compile relevant data for a basic fiscal impact analysis of the effects of preserving a battlefield. This step is critically important.

Develop a Battlefield Plan

An effective plan shows the most important battle areas that should be purchased in fee, those of less strategic importance that can be protected by zoning and easements, the potential location of a visitor center/museum, the routes of walking and biking trails, and the designation of historic roads that should be protected through scenic byways and easements. In addition, the plan should delineate adjoining areas that should be protected to preserve the battlefield setting. This can be accomplished through the purchase or donation of easements, which keeps the land in private ownership and on the tax rolls. As the plan develops, invite public comment through workshop discussions and public meetings. The essence of the plan is to define how the battlefield will be protected, whether it will be open to the public, and how it will be managed and interpreted.

It is beyond the scope of this handbook to provide specific details about developing a battlefield plan, preparing an operating budget, and determining whether a protected battlefield should be privately or publicly owned. Such information is best provided by the NPS's American Battlefield Protection Program and each state's parks department and historic preservation office (see the Resources section for addresses). The American Battlefield Protection Program seeks alternatives to costly federal acquisition of endangered historic battlefield sites. The program, along with its many national partners, provides expert technical assistance and modest financial aid to local and state governments and private and public sector organizations to preserve these important sites. It fosters local stewardship and supports local responsibility for protecting battlefield sites.

Launch the Effort and Keep It on Course

The action agenda spells out who does what and when, so that the effort moves ahead. The plan will require revisions, refinements, and corrections to its course as more information becomes available, opportunities appear, and unforeseen obstacles arise. At this point, amid all the hard work, it is important to keep the larger goals in mind: to honor the soldiers, teach our history, broaden the area's economic base, and preserve the community's character.

Protection Techniques

Battlefields can be protected in various ways. Designation on national or state registers of historic places encourages preservation. Acquisition by public agencies and nonprofit organizations through purchase or donation establishes permanent protection. Privately owned battlefields can be protected from development through agricultural districts, local zoning regulations, donation of a conservation easement by the owner, or purchase of an easement by a nonprofit organization or a public agency.

Acquisition of Battlefield Sites and Settings

Public agencies (federal, state, and local) and nonprofit organizations can preserve battlefields by acquiring properties in fee or by acquiring interests in properties through easements that will preserve the land while permitting the owner certain uses, such as farming (see the Glossary). The following methods of acquisition suggest some possibilities:

Public agencies, when authorized to do so, may purchase and receive land by donation in fee or easements. When purchasing land, federal agencies are required by law to offer fair-market value as determined by one or more appraisals. Sources of funding include on-going programs, such as Maryland's Program Open Space, ISTEA transportation enhancement, and agricultural preservation programs, including state agricultural districts.

- Nonprofit conservation and preservation groups may acquire land through both purchase and donation for ultimate conveyance to public agencies or to nonprofit land trusts that will own and manage it.

- Nonprofit groups may acquire and then resell to private landowners part or all of battlefield lands after protecting them with easements that restrict development.
- Public agencies and nonprofit organizations may acquire a partial interest in land through easement acquisition, which limits its future development; the land then continues to be privately owned and stays on the tax rolls.
- Land trusts can work with the landowners to design and implement a "limited development" plan that preserves the battlefield and concentrates development away from it. (See Appendix B)
- Battlefields that are open to the public require that some land be owned by a public agency or nonprofit organization in fee to provide for necessary interpretation; additional historic land can remain in private ownership and be protected through easements.

There are various ways to finance acquisition of the land. It may be purchased at the fair-market value or, in the case of nonprofit organizations, through a bargain sale (i.e., below fair-market value). In a bargain sale, the owner may claim a charitable deduction of the difference between the fair-market value and the sale price. Owners may also choose to sell to a nonprofit organization or public agency and retain use of the land during their lifetime through a "life estate."

Nonprofit organizations can finance land purchases through conventional lenders such as banks, through grants and other donated funds, or through the owner. Public agencies may obtain land through tax foreclosures or through trades and transfers of property from other agencies. Sources of acquisition funds for public agencies include appropriations from general revenue, the federal Land and Water Conservation Fund, Department of Transportation enhancement funds (ISTEA), and various dedicated revenues such as bond issues, real estate transfer taxes, and development impact fees.

Other Ways to Preserve Battlefields

Local governments may use zoning and subdivision controls to restrict the amount, location, and type of development, if they have carefully defined the public purposes and needs involved and have left the owner with a reasonable economic use of the property. Public purposes may include preservation of community character through zoning and historic districts. For example, local governments may limit use of battlefield sites to agricultural and other open space uses or require clustering of development on noncritical parts of sites. They may require contributions of open space or fees-in-lieu of open space from proposed developments, especially if they involve environmentally sensitive lands, or they may offer incentives for such contributions in return for density increases. Local governments may also create programs to allow transfer of development rights from one property or area to another, increasing development in one area and decreasing it in the other.

Local governments, when authorized, may also enact legislation creating historic districts, historic zoning overlays, or other zoning regulations that recognize the need to protect battlefield settings. Such regulations may limit uses to those least likely to affect the battlefield, reduce densities of development, or require preservation of natural buffers on the borders of battlefield properties.

Section 106 of the National Historic Preservation Act requires that federal agencies (or those acting with federal funds, permits, or licenses) involved in projects on properties listed in or eligible for the National Register of Historic Places consider the effect of the projects on the properties. One example would be the use of federal funds to widen a historic road through a battlefield (also see the Glossary).

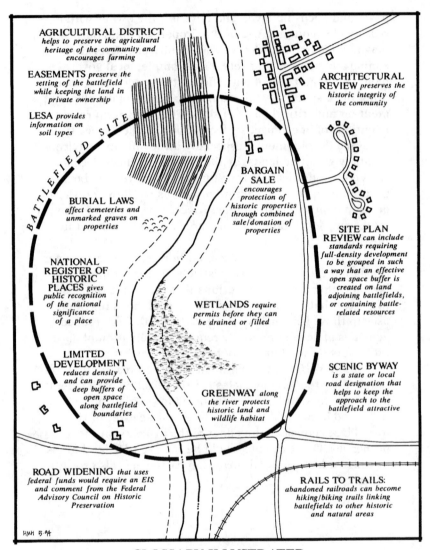

AGRICULTURAL DISTRICT *helps to preserve the agricultural heritage of the community and encourages farming*

EASEMENTS *preserve the setting of the battlefield while keeping the land in private ownership*

LESA *provides information on soil types*

ARCHITECTURAL REVIEW *preserves the historic integrity of the community*

BATTLEFIELD SITE

BURIAL LAWS *affect cemeteries and unmarked graves on properties*

BARGAIN SALE *encourages protection of historic properties through combined sale/donation of properties*

SITE PLAN REVIEW *can include standards requiring full-density development to be grouped in such a way that an effective open space buffer is created on land adjoining battlefields, or containing battle-related resources*

NATIONAL REGISTER OF HISTORIC PLACES *gives public recognition of the national significance of a place*

WETLANDS *require permits before they can be drained or filled*

LIMITED DEVELOPMENT *reduces density and can provide deep buffers of open space along battlefield boundaries*

SCENIC BYWAY *is a state or local road designation that helps to keep the approach to the battlefield attractive*

GREENWAY *along the river protects historic land and wildlife habitat*

ROAD WIDENING *that uses federal funds would require an EIS and comment from the Federal Advisory Council on Historic Preservation*

RAILS TO TRAILS: *abandoned railroads can become hiking/biking trails linking battlefields to other historic and natural areas*

HMH 5-94

GLOSSARY ILLUSTRATED

Glossary

Tools for
Protecting Battlefields

The information in italics relates the term to
battlefield protection.

Agricultural districts: State-recognized areas in which agricultural use of land is encouraged and protected
through various government programs. Owners of
agricultural land agree not to develop their property
for a period of time, usually five to 10 years. In return the state agrees not to extend public services
(and the ensuing tax burden) that would facilitate
nonagricultural development and, in many places, to
lower property tax assessments to reflect agricul-
tural-use value rather than development value. Inclusion in an agricultural district is generally
voluntary; districts must meet state criteria.

Right-to-farm laws exempt properly managed agricultural operations from nuisance suits and local regulations
restricting conventional farm practices.

*Keeping battlefields and their surroundings in ag-
ricultural use will not be feasible unless the area has a
healthy farm economy. Without a critical mass of working farms, a region cannot support the secondary businesses that serve farmers. As farmland is converted to
housing, feed supply stores become garden centers, it
becomes more difficult to get machinery serviced, and*

veterinarians begin to specialize in pets rather than farm animals. Protecting the lands adjacent to, as well as on, a battlefield through farmland preservation involves a comprehensive agricultural preservation plan addressing economic as well as aesthetic issues.

Architectural review: Review of new construction and alterations to existing buildings to ensure compatibility with the historic or scenic character of an area. Architectural review may include consideration of the style, materials, massing, and height of a building, as well as siting and landscaping (see the entry under site-plan review). The review may be conducted by a historic commission, planning board, or architectural review board (as part of a historic district ordinance).

An attractive business district in the town near a battlefield can be an important factor in keeping visitors to battlefields in the area for more than a few hours. A nearby community that provides restaurants, inns, and shopping in a historic atmosphere can turn an afternoon's pilgrimage to a battlefield into a long weekend. There are several types of tools which can be used, singly or in combination, to encourage well-designed facilities.

Bargain sale: The purchase of land at less than its fair-market value. If the buyer is a qualified charitable organization, the difference between the bargain sale price and the fair-market value may be considered a charitable donation that can be deducted by the seller for federal income tax purposes.

Burial laws: States govern the burial and removal of human remains through laws governing public health, sepulchrals, grave disturbance and desecration, and cemeteries. Cemeteries receive special protection, and property owners are required under law to avoid desecration and disturbance of graves. Cemeteries in which the graves are unmarked, the identity of decedents lost, and the remains decomposed may be considered abandoned, and may no longer be protected under cemetery laws. Some states have enacted special legislation to deal with unmarked burials and may require a special permit or court order to remove human remains.

Clean Water Act of 1972, as amended: Under section 404 of this federal law, a permit from the Army Corps of Engineers must be obtained before any wetlands can be filled or drained.

Comprehensive plan: Sets forth community objectives and policies for future development and redevelopment, showing how all the components of development— land use, infrastructure systems, social and economic change—can be coordinated to achieve a livable community. A comprehensive plan is useful for focusing community efforts on current and emerging issues that should be resolved before they reach the crisis stage, by anticipating and planning for change to meet community-wide interests.

Conservation easements: The following information on easements from *The Conservation Easement Handbook* is included with permission from the Land Trust Alliance.

What is a conservation easement? It is a legal agreement a property owner makes to restrict the type and amount of development that may take place on his or her property. Each easement's restrictions are tailored to the particular property and to the interests of the individual owner.

To understand the easement concept, think of owning land as holding a bundle of rights. A landowner may sell or give away the whole bundle or only one or two of those rights. These may include, for example, the right to construct buildings, subdivide the land, restrict access, or harvest timber. To give away certain rights while retaining others, a property owner grants an easement to an appropriate third party, such as a land trust, a public agency, or a historic preservation organization.

Easements often are called by different names, according to the resource they protect. Easements used to preserve an agricultural operation, for example, are termed agricultural or agricultural preservation easements. When the resources are primarily scenic, easements can bear that name. Another term for a conservation easement is conservation restriction. Whatever they are called, the concept is the same.

An easement runs with the land—that is, the original owner and all subsequent owners are bound by the restrictions of the easement. The easement is recorded at the county or town records office so that all future owners and lenders will learn about the restrictions when they obtain title reports.

Why grant a conservation easement? People grant conservation easements to protect their land or historic buildings from inappropriate development *while retaining private ownership.* By granting an easement in perpetuity, the owner may be assured that the resource values of his or her property will be protected indefinitely, regardless of who the future owners are. Granting an easement can also yield tax savings, as discussed below.

What kind of property can be protected by an easement? Any property with significant conservation or historic preservation value can be protected by an easement. This includes forests, wetlands, farms and ranches, endangered species habitat, beaches, scenic areas, historic areas, and more. Land conservation and historic preservation professionals can help landowners evaluate the relative features of their property.

Who can grant an easement? To whom can they grant it? Any owner of property with conservation or historic resources may grant an easement. If the property belongs to more than one person, all owners must consent to granting an easement. If the property is mortgaged, the owner must obtain an agreement from the lender to subordinate its interests to those of the easement holder so that the easement cannot be extinguished in the event of foreclosure.

If an easement donor wishes to claim tax benefits for the gift, he or she must donate it or sell it for less than fair-market value to a public agency or to a conservation or historic preservation organization that qualifies as a public charity under Internal Revenue Code Section 501(c)(3). Most land trusts and historic preservation organizations meet this criterion.

Holding an easement, however, is a great responsibility. A property owner should make sure that the recipient organization has the time and resources to carry out that responsibility. An organization that accepts the donation of an easement typically will ask the owner to make a contribution toward the costs of monitoring the easement in perpetuity or will establish a monitoring fund from other sources.

How restrictive is an easement? An easement restricts development to the degree that is necessary to protect the significant values of that property. Sometimes this totally prohibits construction, sometimes it doesn't.

If the goal is to preserve a pristine natural area, for example, an easement may prohibit all construction, as well as activities that would alter the land's present natural condition. If the goal is to protect farm or ranch land, however, an easement may restrict subdivision and development while allowing for structures and activities necessary for and compatible with the agricultural operation. Even the most restrictive easements typically permit landowners to continue traditional uses of the land.

Must an easement allow public access? Landowners who grant conservation easements generally decide whether to open their property to the public. Some landowners convey certain public access rights, such as allowing fishing or hiking in specified locations or permitting guided tours once a month. Others do not.

If an income tax deduction is to be claimed, however, some types of easements require access. If the easement is given for recreation or educational purposes, public access is required. For scenic easements, much of the property must be visible to the public, but physical access is not necessary. Access is generally not required for easements that protect wildlife or plant habitat or agricultural lands.

What are the grantee's responsibilities? The grantee organization or agency is responsible for enforcing the restrictions spelled out in the easement document. To do this, the grantee monitors the property on a regular basis, typically once a year. Grantee representatives visit the restricted property, usually accompanied by the owner. They determine whether the property remains in the condition prescribed by the easement and documented at the time of the grant. The grantee maintains written records of the monitoring visits. The visits also keep the grantee and the property owner in touch.

If a monitoring visit reveals that the easement has been violated, the grantee has the legal right to require the owner to correct the violation and restore the property to its condition prior to the violation.

How can donating an easement reduce a property owner's income tax? The donation of a conservation easement is a tax-deductible charitable gift, provided that the easement is perpetual and is donated exclusively for conservation purposes to a qualified conservation organization or public agency. Internal Revenue Code 170(h) generally defines conservation purposes to include the following:

- the preservation of land areas for outdoor recreation by, or the education of, the public.
- the protection of relatively natural habitats of fish, wildlife, or plants, or similar ecosystems.
- the preservation of open space—including farmland and forest land—for scenic enjoyment or pursuant to an adopted governmental conservation policy; in either case, such open space preservation must yield a significant public benefit.
- the preservation of historically important land areas or buildings.

To determine the value of the easement donation, the owner has the property appraised both at its fair-market value without the easement restrictions and at its fair-market value with the easement restrictions. The difference between these two appraised values is the tax deductible easement value. Detailed federal regulations govern these appraisals.

How can granting an easement reduce a property owner's estate tax? Many heirs to large historic estates and to large tracts of open space—farms and ranches in particular—face monumental estate taxes. Even if the heirs wish to keep their property in the existing condition, federal estate tax is levied not on the value of the property for its existing use, but on its fair market value, usually the amount a developer or speculator would pay. The resulting estate tax can be so high that the heirs must sell the property to pay the taxes.

A conservation easement, however, often can reduce estate taxes. If the property owner has restricted the property by a perpetual conservation easement before his or her death, the property must be valued in the estate at its restricted value. To the extent that the restricted value is lower than the unrestricted value, the value of the estate will be less, and the estate will thus be subject to a lower estate tax.

Even if a property owner does not want to restrict the property during his or her lifetime, the owner can still specify in his or her will that a charitable gift of a conservation easement be made to a qualifying organization upon the owner's death. Assuming that the easement is properly structured, the value of the easement gift will be deducted from the estate, reducing the value on which estate taxes are levied. Again, a lower tax results.

Can granting an easement reduce an owner's property tax? Property tax assessment usually is based on the property's market value, which reflects the property's development potential. If a conservation easement reduces the development potential of the property, it may reduce the level of assessment and the amount of the owner's property taxes. The actual amount of reduction, if any, depends on many factors. State law and the personal attitudes of local officials and assessors may influence or determine the decision to award property tax relief to easement grantors.

Who has granted conservation easements on their land? Nationwide, concerned landowners have granted easements on some two million acres of land. People who grant easements share a desire to permanently protect and enhance the natural, scenic, and cultural resources of the community. The Land Trust Alliance can put you in touch with your local land trust.

Environmental impact statement (EIS): Studies of the potential impact of proposed projects, including environmental impacts and, frequently, social and economic impacts as well. An EIS is required for many projects that receive federal funding, and some states also require them for large projects that will impact environmental qualities and features. They may identify alternatives to the proposal that have not been considered. Not only do they provide significant information, but their review procedures usually permit substantial input from interested groups and the public.

Fiscal impact analysis: Evaluates the effects of proposed development on the local governmental budget. Such an analysis is frequently conducted as part of a series of studies undertaken to identify the potential impact of new development, including traffic, environmental, and other analyses.

A number of approaches are used, but essentially they estimate the costs of providing public services and facilities for a proposed development and compare those costs to the property tax and other revenues the development would generate. Costs and revenues are usually calculated over the period of development and for some years thereafter. The result demonstrates whether new development would have a positive or negative fiscal impact on the local budget over time. Such an analysis can be calculated for local governments, school districts, and other service-providing entities.

Costs associated with new development include capital costs for new facilities that a local government would provide to serve the development, plus operating costs for those facilities and other government services. Some typical costs include

- improving and maintaining nearby streets and highways to accommodate traffic generated by the development
- providing additional school capacity and services for children who will live in the development
- extending water and sewer service to the development
- providing such additional public services as police and fire protection, local government administration, waste collection and disposal, and library services

Costs are projected for a proposed development by using a local government's actual costs per capita, per employee, or per child or an average of similar jurisdictions' costs. To achieve greater accuracy, case studies can be undertaken to determine specific facility needs and costs.

Revenues associated with new development include property taxes on the land and new buildings, various charges and fees for services, business taxes, and federal and state funding. Revenues, like costs, are projected based on current actual revenues per capita, per employee, or per child or an average of revenues from other jurisdictions. Property tax revenues can be projected using expected values of the new development. One-time fees and charges should also be determined.

Costs and revenues are then compared to show whether the development will generate a net fiscal surplus or deficit for local budgets. The possible effect of either a surplus or a deficit on the current tax rate can also be calculated.

The accuracy of a fiscal impact analysis ultimately depends on the basic assumptions made about costs and revenues attributable to new development, the availability of good data, and an impartial technical methodology and analysis. Although these factors often are shortchanged, fiscal impact analyses can provide a useful gauge of potential fiscal effects to assist in local development decisions.

Greenways: Corridors of private or publicly owned open space that follow streams and rivers, ridgelines, abandoned rail lines, canals, and utility rights-of-way, forming "ribbons" or "fingers" of green. Greenways can connect isolated natural areas, cultural and historic sites, and recreational facilities. As a multipurpose conservation technique, greenways provide traffic-free routes for alternative transportation or outdoor recreation activities like walking and bicycling, while at the same time helping preserve the biological diversity of plant and animal species by maintaining connections between natural communities and acting as buffers for ecologically sensitive waterways. Greenways can also soften urban and suburban landscapes with ribbons of green that improve the quality of life, enhance property values, and direct development and growth away from important historic sites or natural resource areas. Greenways can be established through public ownership or through easements or rights-of-way to private property.

Land Evaluation and Site Assessment System (LESA): The Soil Conservation Service's computerized information system, used to identify lands best suited to agriculture, evaluate a district for viability of continued agricultural use, establish minimum parcel sizes in agricultural areas, and locate public infrastructure projects.

Land exchange: Under °1031 of the Internal Revenue Code, a parcel of investment property may be exchanged for another parcel of equivalent value without recognition of capital gains, provided all statutory conditions are met. This is particularly beneficial if the land has become worth much more than was originally paid for it, as is often the case with farmland in a rapidly developing area. Using this technique, a nonprofit organization can exchange nonconservation land that it owns for land with conservation value, and the original owner can defer paying capital gains tax until the sale of the property received in exchange from the nonprofit. The landowner's basis carries over to the newly acquired property.

Land trust: A nonprofit organization directly engaged in protecting, by voluntary means, parcels of land with conservation, historic, or other public value, usually through land transactions and/or management. Land trusts range from small, local groups run by volunteers to regional and national organizations with professional staffs and large memberships.

Limited development: A technique of land development used to preserve critical natural, scenic, or historic areas by developing the less sensitive portions of the property in a compatible way. Development may be clustered, sited, or designed so that it intrudes as little as possible on the overall landscape. Proceeds from the sale of developed lots can be used to protect and manage the remainder of the property. The undeveloped portion may be permanently protected by a conservation easement, donated to an appropriate organization or agency, or may be jointly owned by the purchasers of the developed lots in a homeowners' association. Limited development can be achieved voluntarily or required by a cluster ordinance.

Careful planning can result in the preservation of areas of some battlefields. (See Appendix B for one approach.)

National Historic Preservation Act of 1966, as amended (16 USC 470, et seq.): Section 106 of this law requires that federal agencies with direct or indirect jurisdiction over a project consider the effect of the project on properties listed in or eligible for the National Register of Historic Places. A federal agency that provides funds, permits, or licenses for a project must first identify any historic or prehistoric resources in the project area, and then must determine, in consultation with the state historic preservation officer, whether they are listed in the National Register or meet the criteria for listing. If National Register listed or eligible properties are affected, the federal Advisory Council on Historic Preservation must be given an opportunity to comment. Many states have enacted parallel preservation legislation triggered by state funding, licensing, or permitting. For projects solely involving private actions, there are no legal requirements to identify historic resources. Private property owners can do anything they wish with their property provided no federal license, permit, or funding is involved.

National Register of Historic Places: The National Historic Preservation Act of 1966 established this list of buildings, sites, objects, structures, and districts that are significant in American history, architecture, archeology, engineering, and culture. Listing in the National Register provides recognition that a property is significant in the heritage of the nation, the state, or the community. The National Register is maintained by the National Park Service and also includes National Historic Landmarks and historic units of the National Park System. Nominations are made by state or federal historic preservation officers and may be prepared by their staff, professional consultants, or private citizens.

The National Register provides a standard for documentation and criteria for evaluating significance that can be used to determine defensible, objective boundaries, independent of current property lines or land-use considerations. Inclusion in the National Register gives public recognition of a battlefield's place in our history and alerts property owners, developers, and public agencies to the site's significance. Listing or determination of eligibility for listing in the National Register does not affect a private owner's right to alter, sell, or demolish his or her property. Projects undertaken with federal funds, licenses, or permits that affect historic properties are subject to review by the Advisory Council on Historic Preservation under section 106 of the National Historic Preservation Act.

The National Register Bulletin 40: Guidelines for Identifying, Evaluating, and Registering America's Historic Battlefields is a valuable guide for public officials and private citizens.

Historic districts. There are two kinds of historic districts. Local historic districts are established by local governments in response to state enabling legislation or by special acts of the state legislature. National Register historic districts are designated by the National Park Service of the U.S. Department of the Interior. Both types of districts recognize historically or architecturally significant areas.

In general, local districts provide the strongest protection for historic resources. Ordinances establishing such districts frequently prohibit the demolition or major alteration of historic structures' exteriors unless the local historic district commission has issued a "certificate of appropriateness." Local historic district regulations are analogous to zoning regulations.

In contrast, a National Register historic district imposes no restrictions on private property owners. If a federally aided project threatens to harm historic resources located within a National Register district, the law requires the relevant federal agency to comply with "Section 106," designed to mitigate the harm. Although National Register listing does not place any limitations on what owners of historic district properties may do with their properties, it does open the door to significant financial incentives. Property owners who rehabilitate their historic structures may qualify for a 20 percent rehabilitation tax credit.

Local historic district ordinances differ widely, but, as Constance Epton Beaumont writes in *A Citizen's Guide to Protecting Historic Places: Local Preservation Ordinances*, they must all comply with state laws and three rules of land-use law:

1. An ordinance must promote a valid public purpose; that is, it must in some way advance the public health, safety, morals, or general welfare.
2. An ordinance must not be so restrictive as to deprive a property owner of all reasonable economic use of his or her property.
3. An ordinance must honor a citizen's constitutional right to due process. In other words, fair hearings must be provided and rational procedures must be followed in the administration of an ordinance.[4]

Specific criteria, established by state or local law or by the National Park Service, govern the designation of historic districts. Some states provide state tax incentives for property owners who rehabilitate structures in National Register or state- or locally-designated historic districts. Such incentives range from local property tax abatement to income tax credits applied to state taxes. Information on such incentives is available from the National Trust for Historic Preservation or from state historic preservation officers.

Historic district designation can mean economic benefits for property owners. For example, between 1971 and 1990 land values in the historic district of Fredericksburg, Virginia, increased markedly over those elsewhere in the city: commercial properties increased by 480 percent compared with a 281 percent increase outside the district; residential increased 674 percent compared with 410 percent elsewhere. In Richmond, Virginia, Shockhoe Slip is a national, state, and city historic district where the aggregate value of real estate increased by more than 700 percent between 1960 and 1990 compared with 8.9 percent for the rest of Richmond.[5]

Option/right of first refusal: Legally binding agreements between a property owner and a potential purchaser. An *option* agreement provides that, for a consideration (payment), a person or organization may purchase a specific property at an agreed-upon price within a fixed period of time. If the option is not exercised, the consideration is forfeited; if the option is exercised, the payment is applied to the purchase price. A *right of first refusal* allows a potential buyer a fixed period of time (typically 10 to 90 days) to match any bona fide offer to the owner for a parcel of land.

Rails-to-Trails Program: A 1983 amendment to section 8(d) of the National Trails Systems Act (16 U.S.C. °1247) provides a mechanism for preserving abandoned railroad rights-of-way for future transportation needs and also allows their interim use for recreational purposes as part of the national trail system.

Real estate transfer tax: A tax on property transfers, based
on a percentage of the purchase price, which goes
into a dedicated fund for programs such as open
space acquisition. Funds are generated in direct pro-
portion to the rate of growth and property values,
which in turn put stress on the resources protected
by the funds.

Recreational use statutes: State laws that protect landowners from certain lawsuits that might result from permitting the public to enjoy use of the property for
recreation. These statutes limit the landowners' li-
ability for injuries resulting from recreational activities on their property. Although landowners still owe
the minimal duty of care afforded trespassers (to re-
frain from willful, reckless, or grossly negligent conduct), they will not be held to the higher standard of
care owed to those who are guests or are otherwise
invited onto or licensed to use the property.

The definition of "recreational activity" covered
by the state statutes varies among the states. The
need for a uniform recreational statute nationwide
has prompted the American Bar Association's Historic Preservation and Land Conservation Committee to undertake the standardization of recreational
use statutes as one of its ongoing projects. The committee will identify the current state statutes and
any problems that have arisen under them, particularly as a result of judicial construction and applica-
tion of the statutes. Working with experts and
interested parties, the committee will then draft a
proposed uniform statute for consideration by the
Uniform Law Commissioners.[6]

River corridor zones: Restrict the use of riverfront parcels
to protect water quality, wildlife, and historic and
scenic assets and to minimize damage from flooding.
Restriction can be accomplished in several ways: by
establishing a fixed setback from the river, applying
an overlay zone to riverfront property, or delineating
a separate river conservation zone. State and local
designation of scenic rivers may also be available.

Saleback/leaseback: In a *saleback* arrangement, land is
purchased by a public agency or nonprofit organization, and then all or part of the property is sold back
to a private owner with certain restrictions (conservation or preservation easements, etc.). *Leaseback*
arrangements are similar to salebacks. The land is
leased with restrictions and/or stewardship requirements; the public agency or nonprofit retains ownership and assumes more of an administrative burden
but may be able to exercise more control than
through saleback. Some of the cost of acquisition
and preservation can be financed through the
saleback or leaseback; because of restrictions, the
cost of the land to the buyer or lessee will be lower,
thus making it more affordable for farming or other
compatible uses.

Scenic roads/byways: A state or local designation of roads
that possess aesthetic or cultural qualities. The designation of scenic roads can help to keep the approaches to a place as attractive as the place itself.
State scenic roads programs generally provide special signage, identification on maps, and, in some areas (such as Louisiana), information brochures.
They may also provide protection from state-funded
projects such as road-widening and may exempt the
road from meeting certain standards, although minimal safety standards must still be met. Locally designated scenic roads may enjoy additional protection
through zoning, which could require minimum setbacks, provide review of new construction, control
signage along the road, place restrictions on tree-
cutting, and exemption the road from standard
width requirements. Protection may be limited to
trees, stone walls, and other resources within the
right-of-way, or may cover a buffer zone or road corridor and scenic viewsheds visible from the road.
Easements on property along a scenic road may be
eligible for public acquisition or qualify as charitable
contributions.
 *Roads played an important part in most Civil War
battles, and many have historic as well as scenic*

value. These roads can be linked with battlefields, historic houses, and other points of interest to form a heritage trail, identified by special signage and promoted through maps and brochures.

Sign ordinance: A local regulation, enacted under zoning authority or state enabling legislation, regulating the number, size, placement, and design of commercial signs. An ordinance is one of the most effective ways for a community to determine the image it presents to visitors. By eliminating the need to compete through bigger and flashier signs, a good sign ordinance can also save local businesses money and put them on a more even footing with national chains. Sign ordinances have been used with great success in historic districts, and signage guidelines have been voluntarily adopted by shopping centers and planned developments to foster and promote a special identity. (Sign ordinances cannot ban signs posted for public safety, such as traffic signs, or apply to non-commercial messages protected as free speech, such as political posters.)

Historic battlefields located in remote areas are likely to be affected by freestanding signs and billboards, which can negatively affect views of and near battlefields. Such advertising can be regulated by local sign ordinances or may be subject to state or local billboard controls. They also are minimally regulated along federal highways under the Highway Beautification Act.

Site-plan review: Involves the siting, landscaping, and other exterior features of new construction. Site-plan regulations may include guidelines for setbacks, landscaping, pedestrian and vehicular access, lighting, and signage. Site-plan review normally is part of the general development review process but also can be implemented as part of a historic district ordinance, overlay zone, or special permit process.

This review can be useful in protecting the setting and viewshed of a battlefield.

Transfer of development rights: TDRs rely on the concept
of severing development potential from the physical
plot of land, but instead of being held by a conservation organization or public agency, the development
rights are transferred to another parcel of land in a
designated receiving area. TDR programs are set up
by local governments, generally under state enabling
legislation, and require a local government to identify
a conservation area where landowners can voluntarily limit their development options by selling development rights, and a receiving area where development
rights purchased from landowners can be applied to
increase the density otherwise allowable. Success of a
TDR program depends on having a strong market for
the increased density and an area that can absorb the
development and attract investment. A modified ver-
sion of TDRs has been employed to allow transfer of
development rights between two adjacent parcels or
between two parcels under common ownership.

Tree ordinances: Local regulations designed to protect
trees significant for their size, age, or historic associations. Generally applicable to trees within a road
corridor, tree ordinances may require that a permit
be obtained before cutting or trimming trees above a
certain size, usually measured by circumference at
the base or chest-high. Tree ordinances may need to
make allowances for the removal of trees to open up
an important vista or historic landscape.

Use value taxation: A program under which land is assessed
at its use value rather than its market value, resulting
in a lower assessment and, therefore, lower property
taxes. In Maryland owners can receive a tax credit for
land protected under Maryland Environmental Trust
easements. Some states have a recapture provision
that takes effect if the land is developed or put to
some other use within a specified time period.

Wild and Scenic Rivers Act: This federal act recognizes
river corridors with outstanding scenic, natural, and/
or cultural values. Designations are made by Con-

gress or by the Secretary of the Interior at a state's request. The act also authorizes the National Park Service to provide state and local agencies, nonprofit groups, and landowners with technical assistance.

Zoning: Discussion of many types of zoning follows.

Agricultural zoning by local governments provides for agricultural use and may discourage nonfarm residential use through such requirements as low density, performance standards, or clustering requirements. Exclusive agricultural zoning strictly controls or prohibits nonfarm use.

Conditional zoning and special permits enable communities to accommodate growth without sacrificing quality of life. The local government may make rezoning of a parcel conditional on meeting certain requirements designed to mitigate the impact of development. Through contract zoning or development agreements, the local government and the developer enter into an enforceable agreement specifying the development, including, for example, the developer's proffers of amenities.

Existing use zoning preserves the status quo by limiting uses to the present ones. Applicants for special permits or rezoning may have to show that a change in use will not, for example, burden public services or adversely impact natural or cultural resources.

Large-lot zoning (requiring minimum lot sizes of one to 10 acres) can contribute to sprawl and inefficient use of infrastructure, and may be considered exclusionary zoning because it tends to increase the cost of housing. It will only be effective in retaining farmland if the minimum lot size is large enough to sustain a working farm.

Overlay zones impose additional criteria tailored to the specific needs of unique areas or resources. An overlay zone supplements, rather than replaces, traditional zoning. An overlay zone for a historic battlefield could include a special permit for changes to existing structures or uses, or a review process to determine the impact of such changes on the historic landscape.

Performance zoning defines permitted uses according to their potential impacts rather than by listing specific uses. It may allow a variety of uses if they are compatible with existing uses as well as with environmental and historical resources. Performance standards and criteria are used to evaluate proposed development according to its impact on the community. It is commonly used to regulate industrial development and typically sets upper limits on the amount of noise, emissions, and traffic allowed instead of prohibiting certain uses.

Planned unit development zoning (PUD): A zoning option that allows more flexible design of development projects while maintaining the overall ratio of housing units to acreage for the entire parcel. By permitting clustering of development, PUDs encourage more efficient infrastructure, lower construction costs, and preservation of open space. The presence of permanently protected open space can be a strong selling point for home buyers. Most PUD provisions are offered as alternatives to development allowed by right under conventional zoning and can be used at a developer's discretion. Some communities have enacted mandatory clustering and open space requirements to prevent low-density sprawl.

PUD and clustering provisions can be employed to preserve natural or historic resources, including battlefields.

[1] Philip B. Herr, *Saving Place* (Boston: National Trust for Historic Preservation, 1991).

[2] National Park Service Civil War Sites Advisory Commission Report, (Washington, D.C., 1993)

[3] Frances H. Kennedy, *The Civil War Battlefield Guide* (Boston, 1990).

[4] Constance Epton Beaumont, *A Citizen's Guide to Protecting Historic Places: Local Preservation Ordinances* (Washington, D.C., 1992).

[5] Elizabeth Brabec, "Does Preservation Pay?" (Scenic America Technical Information Series, vol. 1, no. 4, 1993)

[6] For additional information on recreational use statutes, see Frances H. Kennedy, N. L. Goldstein, and Kathleen H. Telfer, "Recreational Use Statutes: Time for Reform," *Real Property, Probate and Trust Law* (August 1989); Frances H. Kennedy and Gary A. Ritter, "Bar Association Seeks Information on Recreational Use Statutes," *Exchange* 12, no. 2 (1993).

Resources

Sources
of Help

Organizations

The following nonprofit organizations can provide help in battlefield preservation.

American Farmland Trust
1920 N Street, N.W.
Suite 400
Washington, DC 20036
(202) 659-5170

The American Farmland Trust undertakes a range of activities throughout the nation to protect agricultural land. It provides technical assistance to localities implementing agricultural land preservation strategies and directly protects farms by acquisition or other means.

American Hiking Society
P.O. Box 20160
Washington, DC 20041-2160
(703) 385-3252

The American Hiking Society is dedicated to protecting the interests of hikers and preserving America's footpaths. It encourages volunteerism in trail building and maintenance through work trips and maintains a public information service to provide hikers and other trail users with facts regarding facilities and organizations and how to make the best use of trails while protecting the environment.

American Rivers
801 Pennsylvania Avenue, S.E.
Washington, DC 20003
(202) 547-6900

American Rivers is the nation's principal river-saving organization and the only national nonprofit devoted exclusively to preserving the nation's outstanding rivers and their landscapes.

Association for the Preservation of Civil War Sites
P.O. Box 1862
Fredericksburg, VA 22402
(703) 371-1860

APCWS is a nonprofit land trust dedicated to protecting Civil War battlefield property. A 5,000-member organization, the association's primary tools are direct fee and easement acquisition and cash grants to local preservation groups. The APCWS sometimes donates acquired property to state or federal parks, but also manages historic property for public access and education.

Central Maryland Heritage League, Inc.
Land Trust
P.O. Box 721
Middletown, MD 21769

Civil War Institute of Shenandoah University
1460 College Drive
Winchester, VA 22601

The Civil War Institute is an official part of the academic program at Shenandoah University. Its director, Brandon H. Beck, is a member of the Winchester-Frederick County Battlefield Task Force. The institute provides local school-outreach services featuring field trips as well as its regularly scheduled credit courses and summer institutes.

Civil War Round Table Associates
P.O. Box 7388
Little Rock, AR 72217
(501) 225-3996

Civil War Round Table Associates, founded in 1968, is the oldest national battlefield preservation group. Founded and headed by Little Rock political consultant Jerry Russell, CWRTA is primarily involved in leadership activities for the Civil War Round Table movement (begun in 1940) and with battlefield preservation. The CWRTA publishes newsletters, holds seminars and tours, and serves as an umbrella group for people interested in contemporary activities relating to Civil War history.

Civil War Society
P.O. Box 770
Berryville, VA 22611
(703) 955-1176; (800) 247-6253

The Civil War Society strives to keep both its members and the public informed about the latest Civil War scholarship and about efforts to preserve our Civil War heritage. It publishes *Civil War* magazine and a newsletter and offers genealogical assistance to members.

Civil War Trust
1225 Eye Street, N.W.
Suite 401
Washington, DC 20005
(202) 326-8420

The mission of the Civil War Trust is to promote the appreciation and stewardship of our nation's cultural and environmental heritage through the preservation of historic Civil War battlefields and through related education and preservation programs.

Land Trust Alliance
1319 F Street, N.W.
Suite 501
Washington, DC 20004-1106
(202) 638-4725

The Land Trust Alliance is a national organization of land trusts. The alliance provides specialized services, publications, and training for land trusts and other land conservation organizations.

National Park Service
American Battlefield Protection Program
P.O. Box 37127
Washington, DC 20013-7127

The American Battlefield Protection Program, Interagency Resources Division, National Park Service, provides support to local, state, private, and public organizations to foster stewardship and responsibility to protect significant Civil War battlefields and those from other American wars on American soil. It provides a balanced program of technical assistance and direct financial support to those organizations focusing on preservation planning and coalition building.

National Trust for Historic Preservation
1785 Massachusetts Avenue, N.W.
Washington, DC 20036
(202) 673-4000

The National Trust for Historic Preservation is a membership-based organization, fostering an appreciation of the diverse character and meaning of our cultural heritage and encouraging the preservation and revitalization of the livability of our communities. Congressionally chartered, the National Trust offers a number of programs to diverse groups, including Main Street merchants, inner-city and rural communities, historic museum property managers, and others.

Natural Lands Trust
Hildacy Farm
1031 Palmers Mill Road
Media, PA 19063

The Natural Lands Trust is a regional land trust whose professional staff is available to assist the National Park Service in analyzing nonfederal lands identified as Civil War battlefield resources and in developing strategies and cooperative working relationships with both landowners and local governments to protect those resources.

Piedmont Environmental Council
1010 Harris Street, Suite 1
Charlottesville, VA 22901
(804)977-2033

The Piedmont Environmental Council is a professionally staffed charitable conservation organization working with local, state, and federal governments and private landowners to achieve sound planning and rural conservation in the upper Piedmont of Virginia.

Rails-to-Trails Conservancy
1400 16th Street, N.W.
Washington, DC 20036
(202) 797-5400

Rails-to-Trails Conservancy is a national organization that helps local governments and organizations convert abandoned railroad right-of-ways into public recreational trails.

Rivers and Trails Conservation Assistance Program
National Park Service
P.O. Box 37127
Washington, DC 20013
(202) 343-3780

The National Park Service's Rivers and Trails Assistance Program is designed to help state and local governments, private groups, and landowners protect river corridors and to establish trail systems. Projects range from statewide river assessments to plans for a single river or urban waterfront.

Scenic America
21 Dupont Circle, N.W.
Washington, DC 20036
(202) 833-4300

Scenic America is a national organization devoted to preserving America's scenic beauty. It provides information and technical assistance on ways to identify, designate, and protect scenic road corridors in both urban and rural areas.

Trust for Public Land
116 New Montgomery Street, Fourth floor
San Francisco, CA 94105
(415) 495-4014

The Trust for Public Land is committed to conserving land for people through the conservation of our natural resources and the protection of our national heritage. Since 1972, TPL has helped protect land for people to enjoy such as neighborhood parks, community gardens, historic sites, recreation areas, and wilderness lands.

The Conservation Fund
Civil War Battlefield Campaign
American Greenways Program
1800 North Kent Street, Suite 1120
Arlington, VA 22209
(703) 525-6300

The Conservation Fund, a national land conservation organization, creates partnerships with corporations, foundations, other nonprofit organizations, and public agencies to help protect America's outdoor heritage.

The Civil War Battlefield Campaign defends the nation's hallowed ground through research, public education, agreements, and acquisitions.

The American Greenways Program helps communities and states establish a network of public and private open space corridors—often bordering rivers, streams, and wetlands—by working with land trusts, other nonprofit organizations, landowners, and local, state, and federal agencies.

State Historic Preservation Offices. For addresses contact:

National Conference of State Historic Preservation Officers
444 North Capitol Street, N.W.
Suite 342
Washington, DC 20001-1512
(202) 624-5465

Friends Organizations

The following organizations help protect Civil War battlefields:

Brandy Station Foundation
P.O. Box 165
Brandy Station, VA 22714

Cedar Creek Battlefield Foundation
P.O. Box 229
Middletown, VA 22645

Chantilly Battlefield Association
P.O. Box 1601
Alexandria, VA 22313

Committee to Save Fort Fisher
c/o Greater Wilmington Chamber of Commerce
P.O. Box 330
Wilmington, NC 28402

Fort Fisher Restoration Committee, Inc.
Fort Fisher State Historic Site
P.O. Box 68
Kure Beach, NC 28449

Fort Granger
108 Gist Street
Franklin, TN 37064

Friends of the American Civil War
19 Hickory Lane
Country Place
Pleasantville, NJ 08232

Friends of the Atlanta Campaign
835 Frank Kirk Road
Kennesaw, GA 30144

Friends of the Honey Springs Battlefield Park
P.O. Box 756
Checotah, OK 74426

Friends of Mine Creek Battlefield
10075 Goodman Drive
Overland Park, KS 66212

Friends of Monocacy Battlefield
P.O. Box 4101
Frederick, MD 21705-4101

Friends of Shiloh Battlefield
P.O. Box 100
Shiloh, TN 38376

Friends of the National Parks at Gettysburg, Inc.
P.O. Box 4622
Gettysburg, PA 17325-4622

Friends of the North Anna Battlefield
Rte. 1, Box 687
Doswell, VA 23047

Friends of the Siege & Battle of Corinth
P.O. Box 45
Corinth, MS 38834

Gettysburg Battlefield Preservation Association
333 Baltimore Street
Gettysburg, PA 17325

Heritage Foundation
P.O. Box 723
Franklin, TN 37065

Kennesaw Mountain Association
P.O. Box 1610
Marietta, GA 30061

Middle Creek Battlefield Preservation Society
37 South Lake Drive
Suite 200
Prestonsburg, KY 41653

Mill Springs Battlefield Association
P.O. Box 814
Somerset, KY 42501

Monnett Battle of Westport Fund, Inc.
CWRT of Kansas City
1130 Westport Road
Kansas City, MO 64111

Olustee Battlefield Citizens' Support Organization
P.O. Box 382
Glen St. Mary, FL 32040

Perryville Battlefield Preservation Association
First National Building
167 West Main Street
Lexington, KY 40507

Perryville Enhancement Project
P.O. Box 65
Perryville, KY 40468

Prairie Grove Auxiliary
Prairie Grove, AR 72753

Preservation of Historic Winchester, Inc.
Kurtz Building
2 North Cameron Street
Winchester, VA 22601

Rich Mountain Battlefield Foundation
P.O. Box 227
Beverly, WV 26253

Save the Battlefield Coalition
Box 14
Catharpin, VA 22018

Save the Franklin Battlefield, Inc.
P.O. Box 851
Franklin, TN 37065-0851

Save Historic Antietam Foundation
P.O. Box 550
Sharpsburg, MD 21702

Sayler's Creek Reenactment and Preservation
11986 Holly View Drive
Woodbridge, VA 22192

Shenandoah Valley Civil War Foundation
114 Russelcroft Road
Winchester, VA 22601

Society for the Historical Preservation of the 26th Regt.
  NC Troops, Inc.
Route 1, Box 144-A
Catawba, NC 28609

Wilson's Creek Battlefield Association
1845 South National
Springfield, MO 65804

Useful Publications

The following publications provide assistance in evaluating the economic benefits of preservation.

Boge, Georgie, and Margie Holder Boge. *Paving Over the Past: A History and Guide to Civil War Battlefield Preservation.* Island Press, 1993.

Brighton, Deborah. *The Tax Base and the Tax Bill.* Prepared for the Vermont League of Cities and Towns and the Vermont Natural Resources Council, 1990.

Bucknall, Christopher P. *The Real Cost of Development.* Prepared for Scenic Hudson, Inc., Poughkeepsie, NY, 1989.

Dixon, John A., and Paul B. Sherman. *Economics of Protected Areas: A New Look at Benefits and Costs.* East-West Center, Island Press, 1990.

Kennedy, Frances H., ed. *The Civil War Battlefield Guide.* The Conservation Fund. Boston: Houghton Mifflin, 1990.

Mantell, Michael A., Stephen F. Harper, and Luther Probst. *Creating Successful Communities: A Guidebook to Growth Management Strategies.* The Conservation Foundation, Island Press, 1990.

Mantell, Michael A., Stephen F. Harper, and Luther Probst. *Resource Guide for Creating Successful Communities.* The Conservation Foundation, Island Press, 1990.

Stokes, Samuel B., and Elizabeth A. Watson, with Genevieve P. Keller and J. Timothy Keller. *Saving America's Countryside: A Guide to Rural Conservation,* Baltimore: Johns Hopkins University Press, 1989.

Yaro, Robert D., Randall G. Arendt, Harry L. Dodson, and Elizabeth A. Brabec. *Dealing with Change in the Connecticut River Valley: A Design Manual for Conservation and Development,* Center for Rural Massachusetts, University of Massachusetts, Lincoln Institute of Land Policy, and the Environmental Law Foundation. Cambridge, 1990.

Publications listed by the organizations that offer or publish them.

Advisory Council on Historic Preservation
1100 Pennsylvania Avenue, N.W.
Suite 809
Washington, DC 20004

Fact Sheet: About the Council. Summarizes the purpose, membership, major responsibilities, and establishing legislation of the council.

Fact Sheet: Council Publications. Summarizes publications produced by the council and lists their availability.

Fact Sheet: A Guide to Selected Key Preservation Organizations. Briefly describes the preservation programs and groups about which the council most often receives inquiries.

Fact Sheet: State Historic Preservation Officers and Deputies. Lists the name, address, and telephone number of the state historic preservation officer and deputy for each state and territory.

Fact Sheet: Federal Agency Preservation Officers and Contacts. Lists persons designated as agency preservation officers, per Section 110(c) of the National Historic Preservation Act, and others who serve as agency contacts for preservation activities.

Where to Look: A Guide to Preservation Information. A reference guide to information sources on preservation and related fields.

Protection of Historic Properties [36 CFR Part 800]. A typeset, easy-to-read copy of the regulations for federal agency compliance with Section 106 of the National Historic Preservation Act. This reprint includes marginal notes to facilitate its use. Based on revised regulations, which were published in the Federal Register (vol. 51, no. 169) on September 2, 1986.

Fact Sheet: A Five-Minute Look at Section 106 Review. A summary of the Section 106 review process, which was established under 36 CFR Part 800. This fact sheet briefly explains the five steps in the review process: identify and evaluate historic properties, assess effects, consultation, council comment, and proceed.

Section 106, Step-by-Step. A detailed document that walks the reader through each step of a Section 106 review process established under 36 CFR Part 800.

American Farmland Trust
1920 N Street, NW
Suite 400
Washington, DC 20036

Protecting Farmland Through Purchase of Development Rights: The Farmers' Perspective. Since their initiation in the mid-1970's, Purchase of Development Rights programs have protected tens of thousands of acres of valuable farmland. To evaluate local economic impacts and farmer satisfaction, AFT surveyed PDR program participants in Massachusetts and Connecticut. The results, as reported in this booklet, provide insight important to the continued development of PDR programs throughout the country. 1988.

Planning and Zoning for Farmland Protection: A Community-Based Approach. This popular guidebook is a valuable reference for communities seeking to identify and protect agricultural resources through zoning. It offers an introduction to specialized zoning techniques suitable to Michigan communities, but applicable in other states as well. 1987.

Saving the Farm: A Handbook for Conserving Agricultural Land. In invaluable reference for local governments, private agencies and individuals interested in land use issues and the conservation of agricultural resources, *Saving the Farm* offers comprehensive information on agricultural land conservation. It provides the tools for implementing effective farmland conservation programs, offering detailed guidance on subjects such as zoning techniques, general plan policies and raising funds for conservation programs. The handbook's appendices feature model policies and programs from California, although its practical models and advice have applications from coast to coast. 1990.

Town Farmland Protection: A Citizen's Handbook for Saving Farmland. Produced in conjunction with the Connecticut Department of Agriculture, this handbook of farmland protection techniques pioneered by land use professionals and public officials has applications for towns across the country. 1987.

Does Farmland Protection Pay? The Cost of Community Services in Three Massachusetts Towns. Working under contract with the Massachusetts Department of Food and Agriculture, AFT studied the cost of community services in three fertile Connecticut River Valley towns.

71

The studies analyzed the net financial contributions of
land use on these towns, which range from quite rural to
fairly urban. The results indicate that residential development costs more in services than it generates in revenues,
while farm and open lands offset this imbalance by providing more in revenues than they cost in services. 1992.

Dutchess County Cost of Community Services Study.
Development pressures in the heart of New York's Hudson
Valley have lead to a significant decline in Dutchess
County's agricultural sector. This study highlights two
Dutchess towns, North East and Beekman, and evaluates
the financial contributions of three major land uses - resi-
dential, agricultural and commercial/industrial. 1989.

*Is Farmland Protection a Community Investment?
How to Do a Cost of Community Services Study.* Because
of the considerable interest in AFT's COCS studies, the organization developed this definitive step-by-step handbook
to the analysis process. For those wanting to determine
the cost of services by land use in their own communities,
this easy-to-read publication is a must. 1993.

American Planning Association
1776 Massachusetts Avenue, N.W.
Washington, DC 20036

Why Plan? A Primer for the Concerned Citizen,
video by Municipal Video Project.

*Conserving Rural Character and Open Space
Through Innovative Land Use Techniques,* video slide
show produced by Randall Arendt, 1989.

Bishop, Kirk R. *Designing Urban Corridors.* Chicago:
American Planning Association, 1989. Designed to assist
communities in producing aesthetically pleasing and func-
tional patterns of roadside development; includes a chapter on scenic roads designation and protection.

Daniels, Thomas L., and John W. Keller. *The Small
Town Planning Handbook.* APA Planners Press, 1988.

Duerksen, Christopher. *Aesthetics and Land Use Controls.* Chicago: American Planning Association, 1986. Examines view protection; building design review; landscaping and tree protection; and regulating signs, billboards, satellite dishes, and other forms of outdoor communications.

Christopher Duerksen. *Tree Conservation Ordinances: Land Use Regulations Go Green.* 1993. A guidebook for planning and implementing a successful tree conservation ordinance. Targeted to citizens, local government officials, and planners who want to know how to write and administer an effective ordinance that establishes a visual assessment process for tree conservation issues.

Ford, Kristina, James Lopach, and Dennis O'Donnell. *Planning Small Town America.* APA Planners Press, 1990.

Inskeep, Edward. *Tourism Planning.* New York: Van Nostrand Reinhold, 1991.

Kelly, E. D., and Gary Raso. *Sign Regulation for Small and Midsize Communities.* 1989.

Murphy, Peter E. *Tourism: A Community Approach.* Metheun, 1985.

Salant, Priscilla. *The Community Researcher's Guide to Rural Data.* Island Press, 1990.

Stokes, Samuel N., et al. *Saving America's Countryside.* Baltimore: Johns Hopkins University Press, 1989.

Land Trust Alliance
1319 F Street, N.W.
Suite 501
Washington, DC 20004-1106

The Conservation Easement Handbook: Managing Land Conservation and Historic Preservation Easement Programs. 1988. This best-selling book is essential for easement practitioners; highly useful for easement donors, attorneys, and appraisers.

Conservation Options: A Landowners' Guide. 1993. This handbook provides straightforward information about ways to protect your land and about the tax benefits that can result—whether you want to pass land along to your heirs or donate it for the use of all.

Developing a Land Conservation Strategy: A Handbook for Land Trusts. 1987. This model for developing and implementing a land conservation strategy, by the Adirondack Land Trust, is designed to help land trusts focus their resources on the lands that are most important to preserve.

Lind, Brenda. *The Conservation Easement Stewardship Guide: Designing, Monitoring, and Enforcing Easements.* 1991. This step-by-step handbook helps conservation easement holders design and implement effective stewardship programs.

Small, Stephen J. *The Federal Tax Law of Conservation Easements.* 1990. This authoritative, readable legal volume is essential for attorneys, appraisers, easement donors, and land trusts—anyone involved in the legal details of conservation easements.

Small, Stephen J. *Preserving Family Lands.* 1993. This brief but expert guide describes how landowners may be able to protect the conservation values of their land, reduce estate taxes, and keep the land in the family.

National Park Service
P.O. Box 37127
Washington, DC 20013-7127

Andrus, Patrick W. *National Register Bulletin 40: Guidelines for Identifying, Evaluating, and Registering America's Historic Battlefields.* U.S. Department of the Interior, NPS, Interagency Resources Division, 1992.

Civil War Sites Advisory Commission Report, July 1993. Available from the American Battlefield Protection Program.

Economic Impacts of Protecting Rivers, Trails, and Greenway Corridors, A Resource Book. 1990.

Gettysburg Historic Pathway Plan. Prepared by the Gettysburg Historic Pathway Task Force, Main Street Gettysburg, Inc., and the Division of Park and Resource Planning, Mid-Atlantic Regional Office, 1992.

The Money Generation Model. Prepared by the Socio-Economic Studies Division, Denver, Colorado, 1990.

Regional Plan Association. *Tools and Strategies: Protecting the Landscape and Shaping Growth.* New York: Regional Plan Association, in cooperation with The Trust for Public Land and the NPS, 1990.

Sullivan, Jay, and Daniel G. Johnson. *Distributional Economic Impacts of Civil War Battlefield Preservation Options.* NPS, 1991.

Waters, Elizabeth B. *Civil War Heritage Preservation: A Study of Alternatives.* Under contract to the Interagency Resources Division on behalf of the Civil War Sites Advisory Commission, 1992.

Local Preservation Series
(available from state historic preservation officers or the NPS)

What Is the National Historic Preservation Act?
Historic Preservation and Historic Properties
Questions and Answers About SHPOs
Questions and Answers About Historic Properties Surveys
What Are the National Register Criteria?
What Is Section 106 Review?
What Are the Historic Preservation Tax Incentives?
Choosing an Archeological Consultant
Is There Archeology in Your Community?

Local Preservation: An Annotated Bibliography
When Commissions Go to Court:
  A Summary of Favorable Treatment of Challenges to
  Ordinances and Commission Decisions
Zoning and Historic Preservation
Subdivision Regulation and Historic Preservation

National Trust for Historic Preservation
1785 Massachusetts Avenue, N.W.
Washington, DC 20036

Available through the National Trust's Center for Preservation Policy Studies:

Beaumont, Constance Epton. *A Citizen's Guide to Protecting Historic Places: Local Preservation Ordinances.* 1992.

———. *Local Incentives for Historic Preservation.* 1991.

———. *Preservation Planning and Growth Management in Four States: Oregon, Virginia, New Jersey and Rhode Island.* 1991.

Cassity, Pratt, and Timothy Crimmins. *Local Preservation Ordinances and Cultural Resources Protection in the Mid-South.* Prepared for the Historic Preservation Program of Middle Tennessee State University, Murfreesboro, Tennessee, 1988.

Dehart, H. Grant. *Rural Historic Village Protection in Maryland.* Prepared for the Maryland Environmental Trust, 1990.

Dennis, Stephen. "Recommended Model Provisions for a Preservation Ordinance with Annotations." Reprinted from *Preservation Law Reporter,* 1983.

The Economic Benefits of Preserving Community Character: A Case Study from Fredericksburg, Virginia. Prepared by Government Finance Research Center of the Government Finance Officers Association, 1991.

The Economic Benefits of Preserving Community Character: A Practical Methodology. Prepared by the Government Finance Research Center of the Government Finance Officers Associations.

"The Financial Impact of Historic Designation." Report by the Virginia Department of Historic Resources, December 1991 (available from the Virginia DHR, 804/786-3143).

Freilich, Robert H., and Terri A. Muren. *Growth Management and Historic Preservation.* Prepared for the City of Atlanta, 1988.

Frommer, Arthur. "Historic Preservation and Tourism." Reprinted from *Preservation Forum*, Fall 1988.

Hunt, E. L. Roy. "Managing Growth's Impact on the Mid-South's Historic and Cultural Resources." Prepared for the Historic Preservation Program, Middle Tennessee State University, Murfreesboro, Tennessee, 1988.

Miller, Julia Hatch. "Coordination of Historic Preservation and Land-Use Controls: New Directions in Historic Preservation Regulation." Reprinted from *Preservation Law Reporter*, 1986-87.

———. "Owner Consent Provisions in Historic Preservation Ordinances: Are They Legal?" Reprinted from *Preservation Law Reporter*, 1991.

Papke, Gary, and Richard J. Roddewig. *Reconciling Growth and the Preservation of Historic Character and Legal Aspects of Historic Zoning and Planning in the Community.* Prepared for the Heritage Foundation of Franklin and Williamson County, Tennessee, 1988.

Petersen, John. *The Economic and Fiscal Impacts of Preserving Historic Open Spaces.* 1994.

Petersen, John E., and Matthew Montavon. "Elkwood Downs: Its Fiscal Implications for Culpeper County, Va."

Prepared by the Government Finance Research Center of the Government Finance Officers Association, for the Brandy Station Foundation, 1990.

Roddewig, Richard J., and Christopher J. Duerksen. *Takings: Responding to the Takings Challenge.* Published jointly by the National Trust for Historic Preservation and the American Planning Association, 1989.

The National Trust for Historic Preservation's Information Series provides concise information on basic and frequently used preservation techniques. Copies are available from: Information Series, National Trust for Historic Preservation, 1785 Massachusetts Avenue, N.W., Washington, D.C. 20036.

Adams, Katherine. *Investing in Volunteers: A Guide to Effective Volunteer Management.* This helpful guide explains how to design and manage a successful volunteer program. It includes examples of how preservation and neighborhood organizations have used volunteers in a wide range of activities. [#37]

Adams, Katherine. *A Self-Assessment Guide for Community Preservation Organizations.* This valuable guide leads organizations through a self-assessment process designed to measure their effectiveness and help plan for the future. Sample questionnaires and instructions for analysis and interpretation are included. [#45]

Cassity, Pratt. *Maintaining Community Character: How to Establish a Local Historic District.* This booklet provides citizens with a proactive strategy for influencing local policy and opinions regarding what can be one of the most important and controversial decisions a community can make—the creation of a local historic district. [#58]

Gary, Grace. *Organizing for Change.* Change is never easy. Any citizen-activist hoping to influence planning decisions in his or her community must understand how that community functions and works within its accepted structure. Five in-depth case studies illustrate how private citizens worked through the political system to change preservation planning decisions in Atlanta, Seattle, Hillsboro, Ore., San Antonio, and San Francisco. [#67]

Goodman, Collette C. (rev. ed.) Stefan Nagel. *Legal Considerations in Establishing a Historic Preservation Organization.* This publication explains the various ways to structure a new organization and discusses tax considerations and legislative/lobbying restrictions. [#14]

Hargrove, Cheryl. *Getting Started: How to Succeed in Heritage Tourism.* This 48-page, four-color guide helps communities combine preservation and tourism to obtain manageable economic growth. [#105]

Horsey, Catherine. *Membership Development: A Guide for Nonprofit Preservation Organizations.* Serves as a basic guide to membership development and suggests ways to retain existing members and attract new members to your organization. [#49]

McMahon, Edward T., and A. Elizabeth Watson. *In Search of Collaboration: Historic Preservation and the Environmental Movement.* The preservation of our natural resources goes hand-in-hand with the preservation of our historic buildings and landscapes. This publication explores potential partnerships between preservationists and conservationists and suggests ways to ensure that our natural and cultural environments are preserved for future generations. [#71]

Mastran, Shelley. *The Protection of America's Scenic Byways.* This booklet describes the scenic byways program at the national, state, and local level and introduces the National Scenic Byways Program established in 1991 by the Intermodal Surface Transportation Efficiency Act (ISTEA). It discusses the formation of corridor management plans and corridor protection strategies, using case studies for illustration. [#68]

Mathiasen, Karl, Susan Gross, and Nancy Franco. *Steering Nonprofits: Advice for Boards and Staff.* Leaders of nonprofit organizations have a host of management responsibilities, ranging from budgeting to personnel to board relations. This booklet explores these responsibilities and reviews some of the changes that affect all nonprofit organizations. [#54]

Meyer, Olivia. *Building Support Through Public Relations: A Guide for Nonprofit Preservation Organizations.* This issue explains how to conduct a successful public relations campaign and includes tips on news releases, press conferences, radio and television spots, public service announcements, and special events. [#63]

Private Nonprofit Statewide Preservation Organizations 1990 Directory. Useful directory listing statewide preservation organizations in each state. Information on financial assistance programs, awards, conferences, and publications is included. [#101]

Smiley, Marc. *Strategic Planning for Nonprofit Organizations.* This guide explains why an organization needs to go through the strategic planning process and provides a model for organizations to follow. The author includes the experiences of a fictitious historic preservation organization to give the reader a clearer understanding of the strategic planning process from beginning to end. [#66]

Watson, A. Elizabeth (rev. ed.) Stefan Nagel. *Establishing an Easement Program to Protect Historic, Scenic and Natural Resources.* Offers practical advice for organizations that want to set up an easement program and discusses the legal concepts and considerations involved. [#25]

Watson, A. Elizabeth, and Samuel Stokes. *Rural Conservation.* This publication addresses the problems facing rural communities as they struggle to preserve historic structures and landscapes and explains how communities can launch a successful rural conservation program. It includes a resource directory and bibliography. [#19]

Wilburn, Gary. *Routes of History: Recreational Use and Preservation of Historic Transportation Corridors.* By preserving for public use the few remaining early transportation routes, we can recapture that sense of adventure and of America's past. Surveys ways of protecting these resources for historical interpretation and recreation. [#38]

Also available through the Information Series:
Herr, Philip. *Saving Place: A Guide and Report Card for Protecting Community Character.* Boston, 1991.

Scenic America
21 Dupont Circle, N.W.
Washington, DC 20036

Does Preservation Pay? Illustrates the many economic contributions of historic preservation activities to increase construction, jobs, retail activities, tourism, property values, and the tax base in communities.

On the Value of Open Space. Reviews several case studies that clearly demonstrate the economic benefits of open space. Also analyzes methods to preserve open space.

Signs, Signs. The Economic and Environmental Benefits of Community Sign Control. Full color video, 16 minutes. An excellent tool for activists, planners, and business persons on the economic and environmental benefits of community billboard and sign control, featuring beautification efforts in Houston, Tex., Raleigh, N.C., and Holland, Mich.

The Value of Nature and Scenery. Covers the impact of scenic and natural areas on local economies from tourism, wildlife-associated recreation, river recreation, trail-use recreation, and scenic byways, as well as the economic impacts on property value.

Appendix A

Economic Development and Tourism

What industry brings more than 74 million clean dollars into Williamson County and continues to grow?

WILLIAMSON COUNTY
TOURISM
T E N N E S S E E

Williamson County Tourism and Economic Development - A Dollars and Sense Connection !

It's a simple equation-a dollars and sense connection!

Multiply the number of visitors to Williamson County each year by the money they spend for food, lodging, admissions and souvenirs.

Make an adjustment to the figure by adding in sales tax generated, jobs created and property tax revenues increased.

The end product: *Tourism-Economic Development in Williamson County.*

As one of the fastest growing counties in the State of Tennessee, Williamson County also has become one of the most rapidly growing tourist destinations in the state. The Tennessee Department of Tourist Development (TDTD) reports in its *1992 Economic Impact Travel Report* that Williamson County travel expenditures rose 6.69 percent in 1992 to $73,610,000. Williamson County travel employment figures rose by 4.24 percent, and local tax receipts by 6.43 percent to $1,400,000 annually.

And these receipts represent "clean" dollars because the government and local tax-payers do not have to pay for the infrastructure to support these activities.

Local economic figures also support the connection between economic development and tourism in Williamson County:

$ The *Williamson County Chamber of Commerce Daily Inquiries Report* for 1993 states that there were a total of 17,984 tourism inquiries for the year, an average of 70.80 visits, calls and letters per day requesting information on tourism opportunities in the County.

$ The Downtown Franklin Association (DFA) reports that 107,500 visitors attended their four annual festivals in 1993. Using the formula developed by the TDTD for day events, $5,268,575 was generated in the local economy from the events.

$ In 1993, Opryland scheduled 34 tour buses from the Nashville-based attraction to visit Williamson County, including historic attractions and the homes of celebrities. According to DFA estimates, each bus load of tourists coming into the community spends $2,500 to $4,300 a day on food, lodging and admissions.

$ The "Town & Country" tour of historic homes and properties sponsored by The Heritage Foundation in Williamson County attracts 1,500 visitors each year. The Foundation dispenses Williamson County tourism information to an average of 20-25 visitors per day during the tourist season from their Franklin office.

$ Historic 1830 Carter House is site to over 25,000 visitors each year from all over the world. The National Trust for Historic Preservation indicates tourists to the site generate $1.5 million in the community by direct and indirect spending and create over 39 new jobs in the local economy. The landmark's "Candlelight Tour" also draws tourists from around the South every Christmas to view dozens of candlelit historic homes.

$ Carnton Plantation, an 1826 country estate under restoration as an historic monument, continues to see growth in its tourism potential. The home, which was once a frequent stop on President Andrew Jackson's travel itinerary, recorded an annual attendance in 1993 of 12,260 visitors, with another 5,260 people attending special events at the site.

$ Williamson County's extensive historic preservation efforts have paid off in tourist dollars as thousands of families visit Franklin's Confederate Monument, a memorial to the Southern men who fell in the Battle of Franklin, and McGavock Confederate Cemetery, to locate the graves of ancestors and heroes in the battle.

For further information: Williamson County Tourism • City Hall• P.O. Box 156 • Franklin, TN 37065-0156
615-794-1225 • 1-800-356-3445

A Summary of the economic benefits of tourism in Williamson County, Tennessee. A publication of the Williamson County Chamber of Commerce Tourism Committee.

Appendix B

Limited Development: An Example

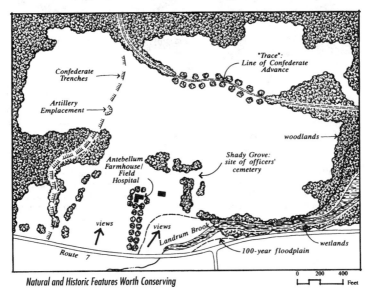

Confederate Trenches

Artillery Emplacement

"Trace": Line of Confederate Advance

woodlands

Antebellum Farmhouse/ Field Hospital

Shady Grove: site of officers' cemetery

views

views

Landrum Brook

Route 7

100-year floodplain

wetlands

0   200   400   Feet

Natural and Historic Features Worth Conserving

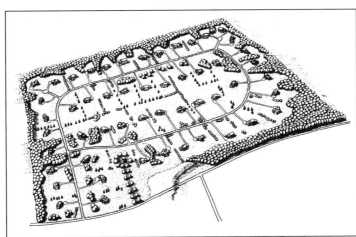

After Conventional Development

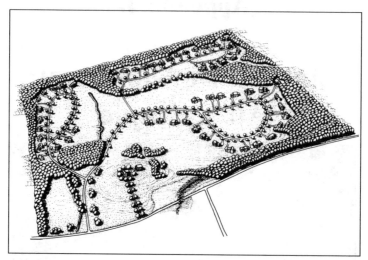

An Open Space Design that Preserves Natural and Historic Features

The battlefield shown in Illustration 1 (previous page, above) would be completely destroyed by conventional development as shown in Illustration 2 (previous page, below). Illustration 3 (above) shows how clustering a similar number of houses, could preserve the historic open space for present and future generations to honor and appreciate.

Site analysis and designs by Randall Arendt (with site plan by Holly Harper and birdseye view by Steve Kuter). From *Designing Open Space Subdivisions* by Randall Arendt, Natural Lands Trust, 1994.

Appendix C

Case Study: A Partnership for Land Preservation - Antietam National Battlefield

The following is an excerpt from the *Maryland Land Preservation and Recreation Plan* published by the Maryland Office of Planning in cooperation with the Maryland Department of Natural Resources.

Since 1987, the Maryland Office of Planning has pursued a multifaceted partnership program for protection of Antietam National Battlefield in concert with the Department of Natural Resources and the Governor's Civil War Heritage Commission.

The Program has included coordinated efforts to protect land through special county zoning, federal park management planning, and the acquisition of conservation or agricultural easements and land in fee by State agencies and local land trusts.

In the late 1980's, the Washington County Commissioners and the Maryland Office of Planning established a Citizens Advisory Board to study the best means for protecting Antietam. The Board was comprised of local citizens, business persons, landowners, representative of the Washington County Planning Commission, the Board of County Commissioners, the Mayors of Sharpsburg and Keedysville, the Save Historic Antietam Foundation (a local land trust), the Superintendent of the Antietam National Battlefield Park (representing the National Park Service), and members of the local chapter of the Civil War Round Table.

The Maryland Office of Planning assisted the Park Service in updating its General Management Plan for Antietam, and creating computer-generated "viewshed" analysis and maps. These were used to identify criteria sites for protection through fee, easement purchase or donation.

Using the viewshed maps, the Advisory Group proposed a series of "overlay zones" addressing the following significant aspects and issues connected with the Antietam Battlefield: protection of tree cover on Red Hill (a southeastern scenic backdrop of the Battlefield); architectural and site design controls within 1000 feet of the centerline of major access routes through and near the Battlefield; and creation of a Battlefield "buffer" to control architectural and site design and to reduce allowable housing densities from one dwelling per acre to one per three acres, and limit certain commercial and institutional uses in the Agricultural or Conservation Zones in, and around the Battlefield. While the Washington County Commissioners rejected the lower housing density limits as proposed, they adopted the other recommended zoning changes.

As proposed by the Secretaries of the Departments of Transportation and Natural Resources, the Director of the Maryland Office of Planning and the State Historic Preservation Officer, the Governor established a Maryland Civil War Heritage Commission in February 1992. The Commission's Antietam and Monocacy Committee, with representatives from the aforementioned local and Civil War citizens groups, is guiding the acquisition of conservation easements and fee simple interests of land within the viewshed and approaches to the Antietam Battlefield.

The Secretaries of Transportation and Natural Resources have signed, and the Maryland Board of Public Works has approved, a Memorandum of Understanding (MOU), to jointly fund up to $12.5 million in acquisition of Civil War sites and Greenways. These acquisitions will use federal transportation enhancement funds from the Intermodal Surface Transportation Efficiency Act (ISTEA 50%) and Program Open Space (POS 50%). About $5.6 million in funds from the initial round of proposals is scheduled for Antietam-area acquisitions. ...

Based on an initial petition by property owners to sell agricultural easements to the State, a detailed land protection strategy was developed by the Civil War Heritage Commission's Antietam/Monocacy Subcommittee. This followed adoption of the new Antietam National Battlefield Master Plan, the historic overlay zoning district, and the delineation of the viewshed and target areas. ...

The strategy involves a strategic process of offering a "menu" of alternative land conservation techniques. The techniques are similar to those discussed earlier in this plan. The alternative choices would be requested from all of the State and private organizations to private business owners on a purely voluntary willing-seller basis, and the menu provides encouragement of gifts of easements when appropriate. When landowners are unwilling to sell only the development rights to the State, funds were authorized to acquire the fee-simple interests in the land, and once acquired attach easements to the land, then resell the land back to private farmers or land trusts to continue its historical uses.

Easements are drafted and held by the Maryland Environmental Trust, Maryland Historical Trust or Maryland Agricultural Land Preservation Foundation, and funded by the Departments of Transportation and Natural Resources. The Maryland Historical Trust and Departments of Natural Resources and the Environment conduct the appropriate historic and environmental reviews. Some agricultural easements are negotiated separately by Washington County and the Maryland Agricultural Land Preservation Foundation. National, State and local land trusts have acquired land in fee-simple to contribute to the National Park Service, or to protect with easements before resale to other private owners.

The partnership approach used to protect Antietam was a response to growing limitations in public funding sources, and opportunity to attract private funds for land conservation, a need to involve community participation in the midst of growing local concerns about regulation and "property rights," and the complexities arising from the interests of municipal, county, State, federal and private parties in protecting the historic Antietam area. There is a surprising consensus in the local community and among all of the players, concerning the overall goals of preserving Antietam.

The overall targeted land preservation approach, has resulted in several successes. These are: adoption of protective zoning, addition of land to the Antietam National Battlefield boundaries, adoption of a revised Master Plan for the Battlefield, protection of significant additional land through agricultural and conservation easements, and acquisition of land and easements to protect the Grove Farm, site of President Lincoln's visit to Antietam following the Battle. Over 2500 acres of additional viewshed land is targeted for easement acquisition with the first round of POS and ISTEA funds.

Appendix D

Essays on
Property Rights

Following are three excerpts from the journal *Historic Preservation Forum* (July-August 1993), published by the National Trust for Historic Preservation as part of its professional member program.

"Property Rights and Civic Responsibility," by Constance Epton Beaumont

Imagine that you live in a community in which you are absolutely free to do whatever you please with your property— and so is everyone else. Your house is situated in a quiet residential neighborhood—until your neighbor sells his corner property to a twenty-four-hour gas station. Your home is a solid investment—until a neighbor devalues it by cutting down all of the trees in his or her front yard and turning it into a used car lot.

Your children walk to school along tree-lined streets—until one of the roads is widened to eight lanes and sidewalks are removed to accommodate a new shopping center. Your downtown, in which city residents have invested millions of tax dollars for streets, parks, and other public facilities, is healthy and vibrant—until the construction of a regional shopping mall out by the interstate kills the downtown because the region isn't big enough to sustain two major retail centers.

Your property taxes are reasonable until the cost of duplicating public structures and services—roads, water and sewer lines, schools, libraries, police and fire services—in the now depressed downtown and the sprawl-

ing suburbs so strains the city budget that taxes must
go up.

***

It is no accident that American communities are
becoming uglier, more disorienting, and more dysfunc-
tional every day. In the past, citizens have been able to
use a variety of tools— historic district ordinances, local
comprehensive plans, urban design guidelines, land use
policies—to determine how their community should
grow, how it can best serve their needs, how it can retain the places they value and want to preserve. Yet
these mechanisms for preserving the beauty, livability,
and cultural heritage of our communities are now
threatened.

The threat comes under the guise of an argument
that sounds plausible and consistent with our social and
political traditions. It passes as a property-rights argument
that runs something like this: My home is my castle. No
one has a right to tell me what I can do with my property.
People should be free to use their property however they
please. If the government wants to impose regulations that
restrict the use of my land, or if it wants to designate my
property as historic, that is unconstitutional.

***

Robert E. Stipe, one of the nation's foremost experts
on historic preservation, observes, "As a nation, we have
always enjoyed the use and enjoyment of private property
as a fundamental, protected right, and we must continue
to so regard it. But individual property rights and values
can exist only so long as we recognize and accept our personal responsibility to balance our private ambitions with
the needs of the larger community of which we and our
property are a part."

***

With respect to history, people take an interest in the
accomplishments of their community, society, or culture

for various reasons. Some are instructional. Others are inspirational.

On one level, we preserve things from the past for purely utilitarian reasons. We record our ideas in books and preserve them in libraries or in our homes so that we and our children won't have to struggle unnecessarily searching for solutions to life's many challenges.

Although ideas can usually be expressed in the written word, most of us find it easier to comprehend what we can see. The preservation of historic sites and structures helps us do this. It is one thing to read about the travails of early immigrants to America. It is quite another to visit Ellis Island and wander through the Main Hall, where immigrants were processed upon landing on our shores. It is one thing to be told that people once got around without depending on the private automobile. It is another to see that even today, in places like Old Town Alexandria, Virginia, people still carry out essential commercial and social activities without the car because historic town planning, urban design, and land-use principles enable them to do so.

In this sense, then, historic places act as teachers and animators. They bring history to life, and they show us how to solve problems.

A second reason for preserving our history is inspirational. Historic sites and structures have a way of transporting us from our world into realms in which we see the value of setting higher goals for ourselves and the possibility of reaching them. We are sobered when we walk the grounds at the Antietam National Battlefield and think about the sacrifices young men made for our nation.

***

Those seeking to dismantle our system for protecting culturally or architecturally significant places often dismiss historic preservation as a mere aesthetic concern that hardly compares to freedom. In doing so they present us with a false choice. To suggest that Americans must forfeit their cultural heritage and quality of life for the sake of unfettered freedom debases the concept of freedom itself. Freedom to do what? Destroy the neighborhood? Defeat the efforts of one's fellow citizens to enhance their community? Squander our resources, both human and natural? Deprive our grandchildren of the opportunity to see and understand the surroundings and way of life of past generations?

When people enter society they inevitably surrender the absolute freedom to do whatever they please whenever they want.

***

Rights imply responsibilities—to our neighbors, to our community, to our grandchildren. It is a central tenet of the historic preservation movement that we have a responsibility to use limited resources wisely, to preserve and protect important embodiments of our culture, and to pass on to posterity a world that is in as good a condition as, if not better than, the world we inherited.

"Historic Preservation and the Constitution," by Richard J. Roddewig

Despite the new attacks from the property-rights movement, historic preservation is on the same strong constitutional footing today as it was ten or twenty years ago. Let me summarize the arguments most frequently heard from attorneys for the property-rights movement. I call them "constitutional myths," and for each there is a simple response that can call the bluff of the barrister bully and shatter the myth.

Myth: Historic Preservation is unconstitutional. Nothing could be further from the truth. Historic preservation, and the well-drafted historic preservation ordinance, is perfectly constitutional. The basic legal support is contained in *Penn Central Transportation Company v. New York City*, the seminal 1978 decision of the U.S. Supreme Court that for the first time clearly upheld historic preservation as a valid component of the "police power," the term that encompasses that trilogy of local government obligations: the protection of the health, safety, and general welfare of the community. Historic preservation has been recognized by court after court at both the state and federal levels as a legitimate exercise of the police power and necessary for the protection of the general welfare.

***

Myth: Private property rights are sacrosanct in our form of government. Yes, private property rights are given significant protection by the Constitution. But are they sacrosanct? Not quite. And anyone who carefully considers the nature of private property rights in America eventually finds an unmistakable truth: A substantial component of the value of private property is created by government action. What would the value of a piece of private property be without the public investment in utilities, roads, parks, schools, fire departments, or police? Or without such regulations as building codes, zoning ordinances, environmental regulations, or traffic laws? The fact is that public property rights are inextricably intertwined with private property rights, and government creates a good portion of value by such things as land-use planning laws, zoning and building codes, and even historic preservation ordinances.

***

Myth: If you decrease my property value even a little bit, that's a taking and you must pay me damages. Untrue. The constitutional "threshold" for having a valid claim for damages is quite high. There are many cases in which state and federal courts have upheld land-use laws that have decreased property values by as much as eighty percent to ninety percent or more. For example, in the first U.S. Supreme Court case to uphold local zoning laws, *City of Euclid v. Ambler Realty*, the owner's property was decreased in value by seventy-five percent, from $10,000 per acre to only $2,500 per acre. In other cases, too, serious effects on value have been upheld. For example, in *Haas v. City of San Francisco*, property was decreased in value from $2 million to only $100,000, but a federal court of appeals ruled it was not a taking.

So the property owner must demonstrate a high im-

pact on value in order to cross the constitutional threshold and have a legitimate claim for damages.

Even the most recent U.S. Supreme Court pro-
nouncement on the taking issue, *Lucas v. South Carolina
Coastal Commission*, reiterates that the threshold is in-
deed high. The Court recognizes that it is reviewing a re-
markably unusual factual situation in which virtually all
value has been taken from the property owner. It calls this
case "the extraordinary circumstance when *no* productive
or economically beneficial use of land is permitted." The
footnotes to the case are as important as the majority decision, and in footnote eight the Court states that "it is
true that in at least some cases the landowner with ninety-
five percent loss will get nothing, while the landowner
with total loss will recover in full."

How much of an impact on value must be shown before the courts will find a taking? The answer is still not
clear, even after the *Lucas* decision. In *Lucas* the Supreme
Court reiterated that this is a case-by-case process. A
couple of things seem to be clear, however, from the way
in which courts through the years have handled these taking claims. Decreases in value of less than fifty percent will
be held by the courts not to create a taking *in virtually every case*. Decreases exceeding ninety percent are likely to
be held to constitute a taking *most of the time*. And courts
will be inconsistent when the alleged impact on value is
between fifty and ninety percent—some courts will find a
taking while others will not.

* * *

What should the preservation community be doing in
the wake of this renewed interest in property rights and
the Constitution? There are at least six lessons to be
learned:

First, don't be bullied by the blustering barrister. Despite—in fact, because of—such recent cases as . . . *Lucas*
the law is on our side.

Second, get sound legal advice. City and village attorneys sometimes don't have enough experience with preservation (or even land-use) legal issues to be of much help.
Call the office of the general counsel of the National Trust

or your state historic preservation office for advice. They can at least set the record straight and often can give you good ammunition for a sound legal response to the blustering barrister.

Third, make sure your preservation ordinance has sound administrative processes. Make sure property owners are treated fairly.

Fourth, consider adding a process for considering economic hardship and granting certificates of economic hardship.

Fifth, create a package of local incentives for relieving the potential hardship that can sometimes result from denial of alteration or demolition permits. This can be as simple as creating a small revolving fund for low-interest loans for proper restoration/rehabilitation of historic structures.

Sixth, proceed slowly in your efforts to establish strong protection for designated historic resources. Build political support before you try "state-of-the-art" preservation techniques. Although the preservation commission may see through the bluster of a bullying barrister, the city council may not unless the benefits of preservation have been clearly demonstrated to the local government leaders.

"Property Rights/Property Values," by Donovan D. Rypkema

Those seeking to rezone their property (or oppose historic districting, environmental restrictions, etc.) often proclaim some divine right to use their property to its highest and best use. Based on their orations, one could quickly reach the conclusion that highest and best use means the greatest return imaginable. That simply is not so. *Highest and best use* is a real estate appraisal term that has a very specific definition: Highest and best use is the use that, at the time of the appraisal, is the most profitable likely use to which the property may be placed. The word "likely" is key here. The first constraint on likelihood is what is legally permitted—i.e., what is allowed under land-use limitations. It would be a fundamental violation of appraisal practice to estimate the value of the property assuming a use not presently permitted unless it were *probable* that the land-use restriction would be changed. Just the *possibility* of current regulation being changed is not sufficient; the appraiser would have to demonstrate the probability of change. In other words, for the owner of an undeveloped forty acres currently zoned general agricultural to argue that the highest and best use of his/her property is as a suburban office park when that use is neither permitted by current restrictions—nor is it probable that those restrictions will be changed—is very simply misusing and misrepresenting the vocabulary of real estate. Highest and best use is not the maximum value imaginable; it is the most profitable use for which there is market demand and legal authority. If the maximum imaginable value were the standard, we would have adult bookstores, hazardous-waste disposal sites, steel mills, and sewage-disposal plants in every residential neighborhood in America.

Furthermore, highest and best use often includes noneconomic factors.

The most profitable likely use cannot always be interpreted strictly in terms of money. Return sometimes takes the form of amenities. A wooded urban site, for example, may have its highest and best use as a public park; or the amenities of living in a private dwelling may represent to its owner satisfaction that outweighs a monetary net rental yield available from rental to a typical tenant. In this time of increasing concern over the environmental effects of land use, environmental acceptability is becoming an addition to the highest and best use concept.

Land-use regulations protect property values. But where does real estate value originate? Some landowners would have you believe that the value of their assets somehow emerges from within the boundaries of their sites, and that since that value was created within their lot lines, they are entitled to the highest returns available. Nothing, in fact, could be further from the truth. Consider two five-acre parcels of desert land— one in the middle of the Sahara and the other in the middle of Las Vegas. Within the lot lines both have the same physical characteristics: flat, dry, and, in their natural state, incapable of supporting human habitation. Do they have the same economic value?

Obviously not. But the differences between the two lie entirely outside of the boundaries of the property. Everyone has heard the old adage that the three most important characteristics of real estate are location, location, location. the truth of that maxim is well-illustrated by the two desert parcels.

It is not the land but the activity surrounding the land that gives considerable value to one parcel and next to none to the other. In other words, the millions of dollars the Las Vegas site is worth stems not from the investment of the deed holder of the site but almost entirely from the investment of *others*— the City of Las Vegas, employers, owners of other properties, residents of Las Vegas. The creation of value in real estate is to a large extent *external* to the property itself.